THE DEBT TRAP

A Reader's Guide

By
John Champion

Copyright © John Champion 2019
All rights reserved.
ISBN: 978-0-9989990-9-8

DEDICATION

This book is dedicated to the all wise, loving, faithful, living God, and the example that was given through his word, and his son Jesus Christ. Ever reminding me not to judge Christ by the Christian. This book is also dedicated, in memory to my father Ed A. Champion and his mission to "love like a man" in the example of Jesus." And to my wonderful kids Jacob, Loren, Clint, and Sara.

ACKNOWLEDGEMENTS

A huge thank you to my dear friend, publisher, and fellow author Michael Johnson. His patience, guidance and experience in helping me with this book has been more than I can express. As well as all the people that have mentored me to this point: Jon Heratyk, for teaching me about credit. John Weyhgandt for teaching me about debt. David J. Tucker, Mary Lynn Tiegs, Chris James, Al and Juanita Grey, Drew Vamosi, my sister Sally, and my mother Ann for teaching me what the love of God looks like. Jim Maloney, Kash Rastan, and Adam Deleon for financial coaching. And last, but not least, Hope Champion, for making me a better man.

INTRODUCTION

Welcome to the new approach to financial freedom. Where people learn their goals and dreams first and not give in to the debt trap. This system brings people out of the debt trap and changes the culture of their family for generations to come. You will progress from lack to plenty, and from fear to faith. It is our sincerest hope that after you implement the tools taught here, you, your family, friends and neighbors will live debt-free. That you will have enough money in the bank to cover emergencies and provide for your loved ones, without having to go into debt.

CONTENTS

INTRODUCTION		5
FORWARD		9
SECTION ONE:	**DEBT MANAGEMENT**	10
Chapter 1:	The Wages of Lend is Debt	11
Chapter 2:	The Nature of the Beast	15
Chapter 3:	Finances 101	18
Chapter 4:	The Genesis of the Banking System	23
Chapter 5:	There is a Solution	29
Chapter 6:	The Golden Rule	33
Chapter 7:	Keeping up with the Joneses	45
Chapter 8:	Health is Wealth	52
Chapter 9:	Enough is Enough	56
Chapter 10:	Re-humanization	61
Chapter 11:	Other Economic Factors	71
Chapter 12:	Critical Thinking	78
Chapter 13:	What Real Wealth Looks Like	89
Chapter 14:	Breaking the Debt Trap	100
SECTION TWO	**FINANCIAL PRODUCTS**	116
Chapter 15:	Life Insurance	117
Chapter 16:	Employee Retirement Plans	127
Chapter 17:	Annuities	130
Chapter 18:	Mutual Funds	135
Chapter 19:	Brokerage Accounts	139
Chapter 20:	Margin Accounts	142
Chapter 21:	Hedge Funds	145
Chapter 22:	REIT'S	146
Chapter 23:	Independent Savings	147
Chapter 24:	The Greatest Investment	150

:

ILLUSTRATIONS

Figure 1:	Favoritism		18
Figure 2:	Institutional Bankers		19
Figure 3:	Big Fish Eat Little Fish		26
Figure 4:	Shark Tank		30
Figure 5:	Foolish Pride		34
Figure 6:	The Face of Arrogance		41
Figure 7:	The Heart of Wrath		43
Figure 8:	Slothful Existence		48
Figure 9:	Hungry Whimpie		52
Figure 10:	Ebenezer Scrooge		56
Figure 11:	Human Devaluation		61
Figure 12:	Peppy La Pew		63
Figure 13:	The Faces of Envy		67
Figure 14:	The Silent Predator		71
Figure 15:	Financial Services Licenses		72
Figure 16:	The True Cost of College		73
Figure 17:	Failing to Plan		75
Figure 18:	Brain Waves		82
Figure 19:	The Game of Life		101
Figure 20:	Quit Playing the Rigged Game		124
Figure 21:	The X-curve		125
Figure 22:	Term Plus Perm		140
Figure 23:	Stops and Limits		143
Figure 24:	Options Matrix		148
Figure 25:	Personal Investment House		150
Figure 26:	Shared Wealth BIG YOU – little them		153

TABLES

Table 1:	Payoff Loan	20
Table 2:	Monthly Budget	55
Table 3:	Opportunity Costs	75
Table 4:	Family Balance Sheet	95
Table 5:	Family Goals	98
Table 6:	Limits on Employee Retirement Contributions	127
Table 7:	Tax Deferred vs. Tax Free	128
Table 8:	Employees Retirement Plan Comparisons	128

FORWARD

The debt trap starts innocently enough. People just want to have a happy life. But they get sucked into a system that only seems to support their happiness. They get a job that earns them money. But they spend it on bills that escalate with their social status. Or, they go to college and get a student loan, all the time being told that they'll be able to pay it off in no time at all, with their big degree and the new job. Either way, they spend as much as they get, and there's nothing left at the end of the month.

One day an emergency comes along. The car breaks down or the refrigerator stops working. Fixing the problem will cost $500 that they *don't* have in the bank. But fix it, they must. So, they finally use that credit card that was for emergencies, only. Now, they are still spending everything they get, and they have a credit card payment to boot.

Then the family vacation time rolls around. But they weren't able to save as much as they needed. Since the airfare is paid for and the lodging reserved, they feel obligated to travel. So, they use that credit card that was set aside for travel. They'll have it paid off by the time they travel again; right? An objective observer can easily see the progression. But you're not objective when it's *your* family's vacation.

Then the student loans come due. And you're not in the least bit objective. You still have the same income, that you could barely get by on before, and three loan payments on top of that. Then you, or your spouse, find yourself out of a job. It could happen to anyone. The only people offering assistance are the credit card companies. You take out another loan to cover the bills for a couple months, until you get another job. But, for reasons that none of us understand, you don't get the first paycheck for three weeks. Are you kidding me? Another three weeks is another month of bills. If this sounds like your story, you are in the debt trap.

SECTION ONE: DEBT MANAGEMENT

CHAPTER 1: THE WAGES OF LEND IS DEBT

There once was a man — a simple man that lived his life according to God's plan. Of what he earned, he *first* tithed and then saved. When temptation came, he never compromised. With his hands, he made his wages and ignored the world's values, while all of his friends laughed and played and spent their money on come-what-may. The simple man scrimped and saved until the day his road was paved. He lived in peace. He lived with joy. And he didn't need a shiny new toy. In 10 short years his home was built, and he lived well, without any guilt. And all his friends that spent their dough, had to get up early and *go, go, go*.

Bestselling author, Robert Kiosake, proposed a comparison of what two men taught their sons about money. The *poor* dad had a PhD. He told his son to go school, then get a job to pay his debts. But his son never learned how to handle accounting, or even balance a checkbook. But he *did* get a PhD.

The *rich* dad, on the other hand, explained that the education system is set up to keep you in debt. There is a reason that only four states teach financial education as curriculum in their school system. The federal government decides what curriculum is generally on a child's class schedule. The reason there is no financial education in that class schedule is because they want you to be broke. They want you to be an employee. They want you to be controllable.

Think about it. If you're in charge of a society, and you need people in that society to perform certain functions, then you need them to be compliant. The best way to make people compliant is to limit their options. The only way to limit their options is to limit their knowledge about the methods by which the knowledgeable *few* create options.

When I was young, my dad was the president of his company. We had a five-bedroom house with a pool in the backyard for us kids and our dog. It was very much like that old TV show; "Leave it to Beaver." My dad got an offer to be bought out of the company that *he* owned. The deal would've set us up very nicely. Taking a lump sum would have created riches that would generate enough interest for us to live comfortably. Instead, he accepted they're offer of a tenth of the lump sum, each year, for ten years *without interest*.

That income stream was barely enough to support him and our family through the startup of his new business. At the end of the 10-year payout, his new business was in debt and he was struggling to pay our bills. If he had been better educated and knew what to do with the lump sum payment, we would've been set for life.

Then my little brother went on a ski trip. He fell down and had his skull broken by a skier, causing massive brain damage. He was rushed to the Mayo Clinic where they performed emergency surgeries to save his life. As a footnote my brother is okay today and he's my hero. Unfortunately, and without my father's knowledge, his new office manager neglected to pay the company's group health insurance premiums. No doubt it came as a shock to my father. $200,000 in bills from the Mayo Clinic stacked up quickly. He didn't have enough money saved to pay the Mayo Clinic, *and* service the loan on the business.

The banks came in and put a lock on his door and took away his inventory. My father's company, the pool in the backyard, the boats and vacations all became things of the past. Our whole family's focus was on saving my brother's life. We went from the beautiful house in the suburbs, to a cockroach infested townhouse, while trying to recover from the financial devastation. I went to work for somebody else and went out on my own so as not to be a burden to my family.

That was my first impression of banking. How could they do that to a good man? My dad had to file bankruptcy and go to work for somebody else for the first time in 25 years. I drew a picture, somewhere in our family archives, of the bank president sitting there with vampire-like fangs saying, *"Sure we'll lend you the money."*

Being of the same mindset as my father, I went to work and moved to California to further my opportunities. But I still had the employee's impoverished mindset. I got a series of great jobs but never saved any money. As my income went up, so did my spending. Money went out the door as fast as it came in. Since I didn't have the money for emergencies, I had to use credit cards instead. Sometime later I got married. We had four kids in our home — one hers, one mine, and two foster kids that were troubled friends of my son.

As the top sales rep for the advertising company that I work for, I made good money. I carried credit card debt of around $3,000, spread amongst three cards. When the 2008 financial crisis went into full gear it became harder for me to sell advertising. Although, I still held my own. With a wife and four kids, I took my role as a husband and father very seriously. I paid my credit card bills on time. Which meant I had great credit but very little income.

Then the evil came upon us, in the form of subprime mortgages and equity loans. With skyrocketing interest rates, homeowners were strapped for cash. Credit card companies were starting to see people default on loans at a record pace. So, they scrambled for capital to show profit to their Board of Directors and shareholders. They invented new ways to generate revenue. In the fine print of my monthly billing statements, which I neglected to read, they changed my payment dates. And those payments became due two to three days earlier on each one of those credit cards.

I paid my credit card bills totaling about $200 on time, as far as I knew. The next month I found out that they had *all* changed the payment dates. My previous month payments were late. Thus, spiking my interest rates from around 9% to 30%. My minimum monthly payment went from $200 a month to $700 a month. You see, they knew that I was somebody who paid on time, to keep good credit. I was their ideal robotic candidate. That fine print netted them the extra revenue they needed to balance their books.

How could they do this? I was a good customer. I paid my debts and did what society told me to do. I was compliant. But that $3,000 debt quickly ballooned to about $22,000 with the new interest rates. I had to face the hard fact that I was unable to pay the $700 a month they were charging me, and still take care of my wife and children. In essence, the credit card companies rearranged my financial priories to ensure their own survival. To hell with my family.

Not knowing any better and not having the *knowledge* of any other tools or resources, I did the only thing that I knew how to do. I filed for bankruptcy. Ironically, my father was the one who lent me the money to pay for a bankruptcy attorney. And while bankruptcy may be a good option for some people in debt, it is not the *only* — or even the *best* option available. But like most public-school educated Americans, I didn't know that at the time.

CHAPTER 2: THE NATURE OF THE BEAST

After my collapse into financial insolvency, I sought out the root cause of the financial injustice in the United States. The education about money that is given to the top 5% is not given to everybody else. And the top 5% profit mightily from it.

Discrimination against the financially uneducated masses is a gross injustice and the most widespread prejudice that we currently endure. Financial insecurity cuts a wide swath through all ethnicities. Being rich, in itself, is not something to be despised. God wants us to prosper. But if we obtain wealth by strong arm tactics that suck the sustenance out of everyone around us then we are PARASITES. So, I'm going to coin a phrase, right now, that will apply throughout this book. The PARASITIC-RICH are the real enemy of the middle-class poor. And they keep us fighting over trivial issues while they continue to drain our families of life-giving resources.

The fortunate *few* get taught how to earn, save, and grow money. The rest of us are taught to work for the fortunate few. We earn money and spend it the way we're told. We are bombarded with advertisements placed by the fortunate few. They tell us we are nothing, if we don't buy their overpriced sneakers, or a new car that will plunge us even further into debt.

Five years ago, I took a position that allowed me to learn everything I could about money, debt, and interest. I've gained access to the tools that put the bankers' game to work *for* me instead of *against* me. The same education the upper crust gets is available to everyone.

I learned about money from some of the top financial minds in the country. Prior to that, I felt the same fear and frustration that you feel when your bills come in faster than your income. I've developed a passion for teaching people how to get out of debt and stay out of debt. That idea is to live like nobody *wants* to live for a *little while*, so we can live like nobody *gets* to live for a *long while*.

The concept of saving more than you spend can be applied to your life if you are willing to do an honest inventory of your spending habits. The idea of *realistically* looking at your financial situation is crucial. You must analyze and understand your current situation, if you are ever going to achieve your goals. My intention — my soul purpose for writing this book is to give you the tools and education to change your financial situation for the better, should you want to.

The idea is that financial freedom should be determined by one's ability to make decisions based on a spirit of love, and a desire to help families and mankind in general — as opposed to making decisions based solely on their bank account. These decisions should be dependent on your character, not your wallet size.

Look at these first three cases as an example of financial restoration.

Case one: the middle-aged pastor. This individual was a client of mine that took out student loans to get his divinity degree 25 years ago. He has been the pastor of a very small church ever since. The pastor is raising a family of five on a very small income. He had been paying almost $300 a month — when he could, towards his student loans since he graduated. The original balance was around $21,000. And after paying as much as he could for 25 years, his balance was $32,000 when he finally came to my office. The interest on the loans was accumulating faster than he could pay.

We were able to find a Department of Education program that offered him a $45 monthly payment, for 10 more years. and then it will be done. No more payments. How come he didn't know about the program? The lenders and the banks weren't going to tell him. And the government doesn't advertise. We saved him tens of thousands of dollars in future interest and penalties. He has since gotten his children enrolled into similar programs. He has also been able to buy a family home for the first time. He's still my friend to this day.

Case two: a young man who was wondering what to do with his future saw a TV commercial advertising a top-notch culinary school. He enrolled, thinking he was going to be the next Gordon Ramsay (I still hope he will). He completed the curriculum and graduated 11 years ago with $38,000 in student loan debt. Not really paying attention to the fine print, he did not notice that the interest rate was 12.5%. Since graduation — for the last 10 years he's been paying between $300 and $900 a month on the student loans. With a few seasons of not being able to pay all, the balance still accumulated. By the time I got to him he owed $49,000 on a $38,000 loan.

We calculated how much more he would pay, at his current interest rate and principal. With his current payment agreement, he would pay a another $76,000. That's on top of what he already paid over the last ten years. Mind you, that degree got him a $39,000 a year job. He felt hopeless and suicidal. We negotiated his debt away, for a monthly payment of around $200, for the next five years. He is hopeful that he and his wife will be out of the hole and able to start a family soon.

Case three: a young lady with no financial competency, got married and had a family. Both her and her husband worked hard. But they spent everything they earned and never had any savings. Every time there was an emergency, they leaned on credit to take care of it. Their credit cards became valuable to them because they were the only means to handle emergencies.

By the time I got to them, they had $42,000 in credit card debt. They were paying $1100 month, at 29% interest. Our calculations showed that they would pay another $83,000 on their current path to cover what was originally about $31,000 worth of products and services. We got them into a $600 a month payment for five years. That will get them out from underneath their credit card debt for about $27,000, going forward.

This book will outline a three-fold approach to financial freedom. First, I will explain why people — including myself, end up in these debt-trap situations. Secondly, I'll show you the tools that will get you out of the debt trap. And finally, I'll teach the skills to make sure you never end up in that situation again. Hopefully this education will change your family's culture for generations to come.

CHAPTER 3: FINANCES 101

Trap One: Industry Bias

Figure 1: Favoritism

The financial services Industry, as we know it, will not even deal with you unless you have $200,000 in liquid investable assets. You will not get a call from the big financial companies to help you manage your investments. In fact, they tell their agents and brokers to ignore you if you do not have that $200,000 because it's not profitable *to them*. Emails have surfaced showing major financial groups telling their agents that they would be fired, or reassign, if they offered to help what they call *the working poor*. That's not where the profits are. ignoring 95% of the population is a financial injustice.

Trap Two: Commercialized Banking

Figure 2: Institutionalized Banking

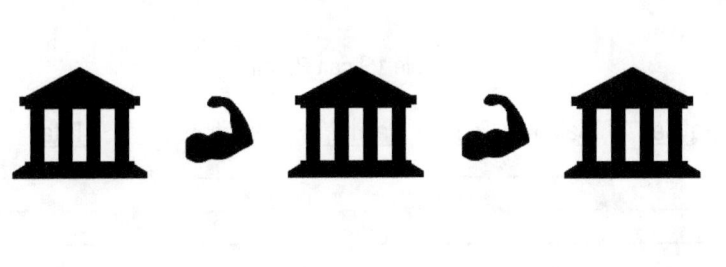

Commercialized banking has the effect of linking our economy to tax revenues generated by big companies that generate debt. It has become common culture with the popular commercials. You know the ones: *What's in your wallet? Get free miles. Get 10% off by switching credit cards. Get the student loan now and worry about paying for it later.* Feel good now and let the consequences be damn. We got this way because people weren't paying attention to the cost of debt.

If there's anything that I hope you will learn from this book, it is the cost of borrowing. Profits are rarely made by a company selling you a product or service. Profits are made from attaching debt to that product or service. Car dealerships run your credit and shop you around to several different lenders to find the one that will give them the most profit on your financing.

It's the same with real estate and mortgage companies. They — or any other industry that sells its products or services, get parasitically rich by attaching debt to your purchase. Ever notice the frown on their faces when you pay in cash?

So, let's evaluate the cost of *your* debt. You're going to list *all* of your debts; cars, house, credit cards, student loans . . . etc., in the table on the following page.

For each loan, enter the following in the first four columns:

1) Who you owe
2) Loan Balance
3) Interest Rate
4) Payment

Table 1: Loan Payoff

Payee	Balance	% Int	Payment	Duration	Total
_____	_____	_____	_____	_____	_____
_____	_____	_____	_____	_____	_____
_____	_____	_____	_____	_____	_____
_____	_____	_____	_____	_____	_____
_____	_____	_____	_____	_____	_____
_____	_____	_____	_____	_____	_____
_____	_____	_____	_____	_____	_____
_____	_____	_____	_____	_____	_____
_____	_____	_____	_____	_____	_____
_____	_____	_____	_____	_____	_____

Then go to my website, getoutofdebtexperts.com, to help you calculate the cost of your debt. When you get there, go to the ribbon across the top of the page and click on financial quote calculators. Then click on the debt calculator on the drop-down menu. Enter the items, one at a time, from your list. Press the calculate button. The calculator will show you how long, in months and years, it will take to pay off the loan. And, the total amount, at payoff.

Add up the total debt balance (column 2).   Enter that here _____
Add up the total to be paid off (column 6).   Enter that here _____
Now subtract Debt Balance from Payoff Total.   Enter that here _____
The last entry is the total cost of all your loans.
Are you shocked; yes or no?   Enter that here _____

The first time I ran my own numbers, I was blown away at how profitable I was to my credit card companies and car dealerships and so on. I didn't understand why banks were so quick to offer me cookies, coffee, and big smiles when I came in the door. So, if not understanding the cost of your loans has put you in a debt trap, congratulations — now you know. Someone once said that ignorance is bliss. In the case of debt and credited money ignorance will cost you dearly.

So, ask yourself this question. If you knew, ahead of time, how much that first loan would end up costing you; would you have gone through with it? The next question is this. If you didn't have to pay all that money in interest over time, but invested the same amount at about 6% interest, what would your balance sheet look like at the end of the same timeframe it would take to pay off your debt?

Here's the next assignment. Referring to Table 1, find the debt that had the longest amount of time to pay back. Now divide the total calculated interest (payoff total minus balance) by the number of months it will take to pay it off. This should tell you exactly how much you'll be paying just in interest on that particular debt every month. Enter it here: _____

Go back to the financial calculators on my website. Under the drop-down menu click on savings calculator. Now take that monthly amount you just entered and put it into the savings calculator, as the amount of monthly interest you're going to save. Then put in the interest rate at 6%. Now enter the number of months that it would have taken to pay off the debt. Enter the amount of money you would have accumulated, here: _____

Interest working for you, instead of against you, is a powerful role reversal. But you won't realize it if you are always in debt. So, you can have a cool car and every new gadget under the sun. And you can overpay for them *forever*. Or, you can save for 20 years and buy whatever you want *forever*.

This is the secret that your debtors want to keep hidden. They keep you in the dark by keeping you too broke to save or invest. Many Americans die in debt. And their funeral puts their loved ones in debt. Debt is a family curse because the financially illiterate teach their bad habits to their children. It's time to break the curse.

Now let's play *who wants to be a millionaire?* Change the interest rate to 9% or 12% on the same savings and see what happens. Up the amount of savings per month for that timeframe by $20, or $30, until you find out how much you would have to save to be a millionaire.

Later in this book we will teach you some of the concepts that help get people there faster. And once there, they can keep them and their family there, forever.

CHAPTER 4: GENESIS OF THE BANKING SYSTEM

The commercialized banking system has set up a process by which they use your credit score as leverage to get you, and keep you, in debt. Because that is, in fact, the only leverage they have to collect on many of these debts. But let's go back to the beginning.

That first bank started about 680bc. Up until that time it was okay to lend people money, but it was considered criminal to charge interest. In the Old Testament, the Jews were allowed to give each other money, and even charge a small fee. But they were never allowed to charge interest. They also coined the phrase; "neither a lender nor a borrower be."

It was the community's job to make sure that nobody ended up in debt. And if somebody did, they were legally required to forget that debt every seven years. The Jews also had something called 'the family inheritance.' The family inheritance was the property that them and their family lived on. They believed that the family inheritance could never be risked, long-term. And that the children should never pay for the sins of the previous generations.

Say a man who oversaw the family property made a mistake. And because of it he had to turn his property over to somebody to pay for a debt, or to make a living for his family. Every 49 years, in the year called 'Jubilee,' the property had to be transferred back to the family of origin. That would be *after* the person who made the mistake had passed away. By law, the children could not suffer for the parents' mistakes. The Jews got in more trouble with God for not acknowledging the Jubilee than almost anything else.

This brings us to the notion of *good* versus *evil*. And, in this authors opinion, finance has always been a question of good versus evil. It has always been the same game throughout history. A few people at the top of the food chain will position themselves as *feudal lords*. It's the feudal lord's self-imposed obligation to own all the property because they consider themselves wise and intelligent. They believe it is their *right* to decide what everybody who lives on their property should or shouldn't do. And if you and your family lived on their property and did not do what they told you to do, they would throw you off their property and starve your family.

Throughout history, feudalism thrived in Egypt, Babylon, Rome, England, and many other countries around the world. And now, here we are in 21st century United States of America, we find ourselves in a crisis. A crisis so pervasive that it affects over 90% of all households. A form of feudalism has quietly devastated and ensnared hundreds of millions of people in a debt trap. We've been sold the *American dream* of home ownership. But what we've really been sold is a mortgage loan. The resultant crisis is debt. And debt has become the driving force for most of the decisions made in homes and families across the country.

Let's look at the numbers. The average American college graduate carries $37,122 in student loan debt. The average income for a college graduate in America is $50,556. That's just the student loans. Now let's talk about credit card debt. The average person carries credit card debt of around $7,000 at 23% interest. The average car loan is $6500 at 6.5% interest. The average mortgage in America is $286,000 at 4% interest. And these are just the most common loans.

All of this seems well and good. Debt has just kind of been accepted as a way of life in America. However, many people don't understand the cost of their debt. It is the goal of this book to educate people concerning the cost of their debt, and the ramifications it has on them and their family. And furthermore, to show them to make better choices with their money.

Let's calculate the cost of the *average* debt. Go back to the debt calculator on my website, getoutofdebtexperts.com. Again, student loan average is 37,000 at an average interest rate of 6.5%. Because the banks care about you, and they love your family, they're going to charge you only $250 a month. Put that balance, interest rate, and payment into the calculator. You'll find that the $37,000 of debt will cost you $74,870 over the next 25 years — that's right, 25 years.

They have doubled you up for the cost of your education. Please understand; we're not saying a college education is a bad thing. But understand what you're on the hook for. And get a plan to get out of debt as quickly as possible.

The average credit card debt was $6,500, per person, at 23% interest. The credit card companies seem to care about you. They want you to have things and feel good about yourself. So, they let you buy things that make you feel good *for a minute* and then they charge you 23% interest. They want to make it easy on you, so they offer you the minimum payment option — only $150 a month. In the end — 8 years later, you will have paid back a grand total of $14,026 for that $6,500. And that's only if you never charge anything else on the card. For most people — that is not the case. The products and services that you bought will be out of date at double the cost.

They don't care about *you*. They care about making money off you. Let's go a little bit deeper. That $7,000 used car loan at 16.25 percent with a minimum payment of $145, will cost you $11,433 over 7 years. Almost double the value of the used car that will be undrivable by the end of the term, without major repairs. So, if you went to the dealership and they said, "here's a great car for $6,500, for $145 a month," and you knew you would pay $11,433 for a car that will need a new engine, would you still buy it?

Now input the average 30-year fixed mortgage in the calculator. That's $278,000 at the average interest rate of 4%. When you run that through the calculator you will find that after 30 years' worth of $1,332 monthly payments, you will pay a grand total of $476,207 for your $278,000 house. And that's if you have *good* credit. The mortgage bankers in the real estate industry are some of the highest paid people in the country. Home mortgages generate massive profits for bankers. Now you know why they are the high-speed movers and shakers. Mortgage debt has become big business. If you knew you were going to pay almost a half million dollars for your $278,000 house; would you have bought it?

Let's get a little bit deeper into mortgage brokers' game. Most of the interest you pay on your home loan is 'frontloaded.' If you owe $250,000 of interest, they collect most of that in the first 10 years. So, you've barely started paying off the principal on the home after 10 years. Assume the house goes up in value by $40,000. Congratulations you made a good investment. it's worth more than what you borrowed.

So now some slick mortgage broker comes along and says, "hey let's go ahead and refinance. Let's take that $40,000 of equity and get you a new kitchen and maybe build a pool in the backyard. It will make your life better. You will have more fun cooking and swimming. Everything is going to be great." So, you get a new 30-year loan, with a new interest rate, at about the same payment. Now you've started from scratch. You'll pay the first 10 years of interest — $250,000 all over again. So, your $40,000 remodel just costed you almost $300,000. Congratulations.

Always remember — you are not the bank's customers. You are the means by which they serve their Board of Directors and shareholders. You are the means by which they turn a profit. It is not the bank tellers, or even the bank managers that are the culprits. They're just doing their jobs. It's a system that equates people to numbers that are the culprits. They don't care about you and your family. They're sending their kids to college with the money they make off of you. And because you gave *them* all of *your* money, *your* kids have to take out a loan for college. Their kids are studying how to keep your money, while your kids are learning how to be in debt for life. Brutal — isn't it?

And lastly, commercialized banking means that the profits in buying and selling products and services is no longer earned from the price of the product or service. The profit is made by putting you in debt — and keeping you in debt. That way they make money off the interest you pay, over time.

Trap Three: You are the Little Fish

Figure 3: Big Fish Eat Little Fish

When you go to a bank teller, they say hello with a smile. They might even offer you some cookies or coffee. They welcome you *and* your money. They make you feel warm and happy. And, yes, I'm sure the tellers and the people that you talk to directly are good people. I'm not trying to paint a negative reflection of good people. Just the people they work for.

So, when you're dealing with anybody that is willing to hold and/or lend you money, the question is who are their customers? Is it you? The first answer is no. The banks managers' and directors' first and foremost clientele is their board of directors and shareholders. Their job is to return as much profit to the Board of Directors and shareholders as possible. You are not their customers. You are the means by which they serve their customers. Their job is to make as much money, off of your money, as they possibly can.

Let's look at the many ways the bank can make money off of your money. Say you get some money and you want to be a wise person. You want to save some of that money. As far as you know, the best place to save money is in the bank. They offer insurance on your money to make sure that you don't lose it. They pay a basic interest rate, so you can earn a little bit on your money. And the money is liquid — you can get it out of the bank whenever you want. That's all well and good, but let's look at what really happens when you put your money in the bank.

Let's say you put your $10,000 into a simple Certificate of Deposit account. The best CD interest rate I've seen, these days, is 2.5%. That interest rate ties up your money for 18 months. The bank then gets to lend your money back out to *you*, and to other customers who have their money there as well. Don't miss this — *they lend your money back to you.* They do this in the form of credit cards, car loans, personal loans, business loans, and mortgages.

Let's start with the credit cards. They sell you a $10,000 CD, and they pay you 2.5% interest at the end of 18 months. In the meantime, they lend money to you every time you use the credit card. But the interest on the credit card is 19%. While they are collecting the 19% interest on *your money*, they are only giving *you* 2.5%. They net 16.5% in the process. And you're thrilled because you got to walk out of a store with a new pair of shoes without paying in cash. How exciting. That's Just like spending $50 in Chucky Cheese, for your kid to get a whistle and an eraser. Your child is as happy as you are, when you leave the shoe store. But at Chucky Cheese it's obvious *to you* that your seven-year-old is getting ripped off. But then again, it's not your child's money — it's yours. Curses — foiled again.

Or let's say they lend that money back to you in the form of a mortgage payment. The mortgage interest rate currently is around 4%. So, they collect a running 4% for 30 years while paying you 2.5%. Wow. Then there's the car loan, where they charge an average of 6.5% interest, to loan you *your own money* while paying you 2.5% interest. These are just a few examples of how they profit off of *your money*.

Yes, they profit off of you — but it gets better. The banks are allowed to loan your $10,000 out nine times. So, they take *your* $10,000 and make 19% interest on nine credit cards — with *your* money. All the time paying you your 2.5% interest. Does that sound like a good deal? Are you mad enough to change the way you think about the money you work so hard for?

You won't learn it in college. It's in the colleges' best interest to keep you in utter darkness. Because if they teach you the real value of money, you'll stop taking out student loans.

They also insure your money, up to $200,000, in most accounts. They buy insurance, because the government says they have to. But they buy the same kind of insurance products that wealthy people buy for themselves. Those insurance products have a cash value side that runs between 6% and 11% interest. So even on the money they're spending to ensure your money they're earning money. And, one more time, how much are they paying you back if you have your money in a CD? That's the good news.

The bad news is that most of us don't even have CD's. What is the current interest in your savings and checking accounts? In most cases it's far less than 1%. At the end of the day, you are just the means by which they make money for the Board of Directors and shareholders.

CHAPTER 5: THERE IS A SOLUTION

What would happen if we could cut the banks out of the picture? Let's say *you* take *your money* and save it in one of those policies that the bank purchases? And instead of earning less than 1%, you earn the 6% that the bank gets on their investments. And if you need your money you can take it all out tax-free. Wouldn't that be better, overall?

In some cases, the banks might even sell you some of these products themselves. But these products *are not* bank products. They are products offered by major insurance companies. If the bankers sell you these products, they not only earn commissions, they get to use that money as working capital that they can borrow against.

What would happen if *your money* was in *your policy* that *you* could borrow against *any time* you wanted to — and pay *yourself* back with interest, instead of the paying the bank back with interest? Can that be done? Of course. It's very simple for the people that know how.

Trap Four: The Credit Score Scam — Smoke and Mirrors

Figure 4: The Shark Tank

    The people who charge you interest, and profit from your lack of knowledge, have to figure out a way to get you to except the weight of their burden. *And*, to make you think they are doing you a favor. How can they do that? The answer is by putting your *focus on* your *credit score* and taking your *focus off* of the *credit cost*. Smoke and mirrors. Slight of hand. Look over there while I pick your pocket.

    Before starting my own credit repair business, I had the opportunity to work at another credit repair company. I learned the different factors involved in getting and maintaining a good credit score. Your credit score is how the bank bullies intimidate you into paying the interest that they want you to pay — for as long as they want you to pay it. Your credit score is based on your willingness and ability to pay interest.

If you're buying a house and you have good credit, you'll get that 4% interest rate. *Because* you have good credit, the banks know that they have a better than average chance to collect the full 30 years of 4% interest. They know that they are going to collect about $370,000 in interest, on your $400,000 house, over the next 30 years,

But If you have bad credit, they will give you a higher interest rate, because there is a larger chance of you defaulting on the loan, before the 30 years. At 5% interest on the same house, they're going to double you up in the total amount of money you'll pay, if you last the whole 30 years. But if you default on the loan, or sell, or refinance before they collect all their interest (usually in the first 10 years) they are still going to collect a very sizable amount of money, from the interest you've already paid. And, in many cases, they force you to buy mortgage insurance to cover their loss.

Your credit score is based wholly on your ability, and willingness, to pay interest on debt. Your good credit score is like blood in the water to hungry sharks. And because people have failed to save money, and have no working capital for emergencies, they have become dependent on credit and credit cards, to handle whatever circumstances life throws at them. They are at the mercy of the banks. So, they try to protect their credit score *at all costs*, because credit is the only means by which they can pay for unexpected, but necessary expenditures.

Once somebody is in this predatory environment, it's usually only a matter of time before their credit score gets trashed anyway. They cannot keep up with the debt. It's a trap — like quicksand. Eventually they get sucked under. These are the people that I love to help. This is the person *I* was. These are the people that are most in need of the education I offer.

So, the main question here is what's more important; your home and your family? Or the banks Board of Directors', shareholders', CEOs' and presidents' second and third homes? Are their families more important to you than your own family?

There was a time in this country, when friends, family, churches and neighbors saw it as their mission to make sure that nobody in their neighborhood, community, or family would ever be in that situation. There was a time when all those things were more important than their credit score. We can get back there — a family at a time.

To summarize this chapter; when you invite debt into your lives, offered by people that profit from your ignorance, you are inviting a wolf in sheep's clothing into your home. Once they're in, they can fully devour any hope for a secure future for your family. When you prioritize your savings account over your credit score, this situation can be rectified.

CHAPTER 6: THE GOLDEN RULE

This is where the golden rule applies more than ever. This author is a man of faith, who believes that the golden rule is the most important principle that you could ever live by. The golden rule states that you should love God before all others — with all your heart, mind, and soul, and love your neighbor as yourself.

In breaking down the golden rule, the first part is what *we* should do. The second part is how to treat our neighbors. And the third part, is the thought process by which you achieve the first two parts.

Golden rule – Part One

Say *someone* makes a bad choice — as we all do, and *you* get hurt in the process. Consider how *you* would want to be treated when *you* make a mistake. Do you want to be judged? Do you want somebody to decide that you are the sum total of your mistakes, and never let you be anything other than the mistakes you made? Or would you like the opportunity to set the matter straight and be forgiven? If that is how you would like to be treated, then that's how you should treat your neighbors, your friends, and your community.

The point of the matter is that you should model, for your family, neighbors, and community the behavior that demonstrates the way you would like to be treated. If you want unconditional love for yourself, then give it to those that you would expect it from.

If you ignore those in your immediate vicinity when they are in need, don't get butt hurt if they don't come to your rescue when you're in need. When you've contributed to the community, Divine Law will return those same things to you. Which leads to Trap five.

Trap Five: Pride

Figure 5: Foolish Pride

Boy do we have this one twisted. Pride manifests itself as rampant individualism. We act as if we should know everything, be everything and do everything, without needing help from anybody. You can see pride all around you. Some people start almost every sentence with the word *I*. With those people, 90% of the conversation is about themselves.

Pride also manifests itself with masks. We choose to put on those masks because we think society demands it. Our masks make our outsides look good, so people will not judge our insides. The masks show people that we do not need — or want *anything* from *anybody*. But we were never meant to be all, do all, and know all. Successful people had help from other successful people. Help in the forms of trust, loyalty, advice and assistance.

This is a deeply personal issue for me. The only financial advice I was ever given by my parents was to go to school and go to work. They told me I should go to college. Not one time did anybody show me how to do anything other than that. To be fair, they had their own priorities, like taking care of my brother who almost died, and building up their own careers. Our family resources were stripped down to the point where it was very difficult for them to take the time, energy, or money to teach me anything.

At issue, here, is your personal responsibility to master something that feeds you and your family for a lifetime, and then to help those less fortunate learn how to do the same — beginning to end. I'm going to ask some hard questions now.

1) What is your area of mastery?
2) Do you have a viable skill that is worthy of being taught to someone?
3) If not, how do you gain one?
4) If so, who are you personally obligated to teach these skills to?

A chain is only as strong as its weakest link. Who is your weakest link? Who is responsible for strengthening that weak link?

My parents divorced, after my little brother almost died. And after we'd lost everything, I put on the mask of self-reliance. I figured my family members had their own problems. They didn't need my problems stacked on top. I was emotionally torn up on the inside. And I had no clue as to how to deal with those feelings. I got down on my knees and prayed to God that I would never need anyone — ever again. If this is what community felt like, I wanted nothing to do with it.

Then I discovered alcohol. When I was drunk, I didn't care about what anybody else thought or felt. I didn't even care about what *I* thought or felt. It became the only tool I had to deal with life. It was the only thing that made me feel any happiness or peace. They call alcohol 'spirits' for a reason. Alcohol made me feel like I could do anything and be anything. But mostly it made me feel like I could keep on that mask of independence — that evil spirit of pride.

One of the big manifestations of pride is the idea that our families are a burden, instead of a blessing. How many massive houses remain barely occupied because people want to show that they are independent? How many people live alone because the world might find out that they are flawed? Since we are all flawed, it is silly to put on a mask.

When we're consumed by pride, we will not reach out to anybody for help — not for anything. We most certainly won't ask for help with our finances. People have become so embarrassed by their financial situations, that they choose to suffer alone, rather than burden the people they love with their problems. That is not love at all — it's pride. And the debt grows on.

Pride manifests itself as rampant individualism. Children move out of their parents houses before they can afford it. Husband-and-wife divorce because they can't work through their financial issues. For some reason they see themselves financially stronger *apart* than they are together. They forget first grade arithmetic: one plus one equals two, and one minus one equals zero.

With this rampant pride in individualism, I see a lot of companies, churches, civic leaders, abdicate their responsibility to help anybody at all. They think it is enough to tell them that they should go fishing. They don't tell them where to buy the fishing poles. They don't mention that you should have some bait on the hook. Only that they should go fishing on their own. These aristocrats don't feel any responsibility to actually show the average citizen *how* to fish.

In many cases we have placed talk ahead of action when it comes to our personal responsibility for helping our neighbors and community. In some cases, we — all of us, might throw a fishing pole at somebody and give them some bait. But we don't show them where — or how, to fish. This goes back to the old adage; "if you give a man a fish, you feed for a day. If you teach about to fish, you feed him for a lifetime."

We have a bunch of, supposedly helpful people, that think it is their sole duty to tell people they should take action. We have friends, and family that spend much of their time telling other people what to do. We have leaders in my industry, supposedly helping people by just talking to them. Obviously, this includes me. There are very few people that have taken a personal responsibility to walk others all the way through the process of learning good stewardship over their family's assets.

Let's look at the math behind the financial woes of individualism. Most of us have a mortgage or rent payment. Most of us want utilities; electricity, cable service, water, gas, trash removal and so on. When the family lives *united*, without pride, there is only one set of bills. If everything the family earns is considered part of the family, and all of the money is pooled together for the sake of the family, then the bills are fairly easily managed. It will not be hard to amass a family fortune, when everybody's income is working together to achieve that goal.

Let's say a family's bills total $3000 a month. Let us assume that there is a working husband, a working wife, and two working children. The husband's net income is $3,000 a month. The wife's net income is $2,000 a month. Each of the children's net income is $1000 a month. So combined, the families net income is $7,000. The bills are only $3000. Leaving $4,000 a month profit. If the family would just save 2,200 per month of that profit for 10 years, the family would save a million dollars. Run it through the interest calculator at getoutofdebtexperts.com. Saving $2,200 for 10 years at 6% interest, calculates to $1,016,498. That's a million dollars in ten years.

Let's see what happens when the mother and father divorce, because of pride and rampant individualism. There is still one home, with one set of bills that totals $3000 a month. Now the father moves out and creates a second set of bills that add up to $2000 a month. And that's the best Dad can do because he's paying $1,000 a month in alimony. Because the grown kids don't want to be caught up in their parents' discord, they both move out. Their bills are $1100 a month, each. So, the family bills have gone from $3000 to $7200 per month. Their total income is still only $7,000 a month. They are all forced to add credit card debt to their already precarious financial position. They turn a million-dollar opportunity into a legacy of debt and remorse.

Golden rule – Part Two

The Korean church is one of the fastest growing churches in the world — in both Korea and the United States. One of the biggest reasons for the explosion in this church is their decision to be personally responsible for the overall success of all of their members. When a new family joins the church, they are assigned three mentors. It is those mentors' obligation to make sure that the new members' home, family, and business are solid and secure. They see to it that all of their basic needs are met. They do this because they believe that is what they're called to do.

The giving of their time, energy, and resources leads to short-term hardship for the people supplying those needs. They exchange their resources for the long-term stability of grateful people. But they are also committed to making sure that their own homes and families are taking care of as well. Once the new families' basic needs are taken care of, the responsibility is flipped around from receiving to giving. They will then be assigned a new member to do the same that was done to them.

Golden rule – Part Three

Pride also manifests itself through the need to hide the shame and guilt of our bad behaviors and run from the consequences. Unfortunately, when we run away, the consequences never get resolved. They never go away, and they never get better. And when one set of issues doesn't get handled, they snowball into another set of issues. And the progression continues until an avalanche crushes us, and everybody close to us.

We can stand, and face our issues with the help of others, and with faith in something bigger than ourselves. But not just something *bigger* — something *better*. Something put us here. Our most ancient ancestors did not create themselves. No more than a jet airplane can create itself. You don't have to believe what I believe. But it would be helpful to believe that there is some benevolent and powerful force at work on your behalf.

After all, look at the odds against you being here. 200 million sperm cells jostled to attach themselves to a single egg. Yours won. Now multiply those odds by the number of generations dating back to antiquity. Look at the odds against *human* life on earth. 99.9999% percent life on earth is something other than human. You were not born to a dog or a spider. Look at the odds against intelligent life in the universe. Even if there are a billion other intelligent species in the universe, the odds of them existing are more than a trillion to one. Against astronomical odds — make that infinite odds, here you are reading a book written by someone else that had infinite odds against their existence. Could two people be that lucky. Against those odds it should be easy for you to believe that you were meant to be here. You were quite simply . . . chosen.

Let's look at another way pride manifests itself. Look at those who brag about their achievements. Most of these people are very intelligent and highly accomplished. However, when you look deeper, there were many people that helped them get to the point where they are now. There were circumstances that fortunately combined with their hard work.

Those are the people that think about themselves all the time. They say they've earned the right to talk about what they've worked so hard for. All of that is well and good until you look at the people around them. While the individual themselves have been blessed, that blessing has not poured over to the people around them. They leave a wake of poverty and despair behind him.

I deal with this in certain businesses. When I coach a business owner, we agree that the ideal outcome is that they have a successful company. When I pull into the parking lot of that company, I look at the ratio of *low-end* cars versus *expensive* cars. If I see mostly economy cars, the business is probably not very successful. And while the owner enjoys many fruits from his or her business, the laborers enjoy very little.

The successful company will have one or two high-end cars in the parking lot. The majority of the cars will be quality-midrange cars. And maybe just a few low-end cars, belonging to the newly hired.

It is always interesting when you hear someone say the words, "it's just business." In almost every case, it is somebody that is about to put aside their moral compass to do something for money — regardless of the harm they will cause to the people around them. If you're a thinking person at all, you know that it is never *just business*.

There are always consequences for poor moral behavior. Sometimes now, sometimes later. The bottom line is that someone who is living in pride lives alone and in fear of everyone around them. They can only judge the world from the glasses they see through. They always feel that everybody's out to get them or take advantage of them for what they have. When, in reality, *they* have taken advantage of the people around them.

To correct the pride issue, we need to have a wiser perspective. We need to see that everything is connected. We need to see that absorbing riches unto ourselves at the expense of others may work — for a time. But once the resources being extracted from other people dries up, our fall will be quick. As it is said; "pride goeth before the fall."

Do you understand the basic wisdom of strengthening the others around you so that your home, spouse, community can be a stronger, happier, better place to live? We help ourselves when we help those around us. A rising tide raises all ships — including our own.

This attitude of helping others leads to a stable, strong, growing community of happy people. People that are at peace with their surroundings, and well able to take care of any of life's challenges. Not only because they themselves are resources, but also because they know they are supported by a faith community just as committed to helping *them*, as they are to helping the *community*.

By showing love to others, we set ourselves free. We are going to stand together or fall, apart. The wiser perspective is to accept the riches, that God bestows upon us as blessings, and pass those riches on to others. We should endeavor to take care of our faith, our family, our community, our city, our state, and our country. We should strive to treat our neighbors as *we* would like to be treated.

If we strengthen those around us with our resources, we will find that we will never run out. And when calamity comes, we will have many people who know and love us, that will stand with us against the calamity. If pride is the problem, then charity is the answer. Do you understand the basic wisdom of strengthening the others around you so that your home, spouse, community can be a stronger happier better place to live?

My commitment to you — the readers of this book, is that you will have personal access to me, or somebody on my team, to continue walking you through the process of filling in the gaps, between your hopes and dreams. I can provide the financial tools to help you get out of the yoke of debt and oppression.

Trap Six: Arrogance

Figure 6: The Face of Arrogance

This is an interesting study on arrogance. I have struggled with arrogance again and again. I'm not throwing rocks from the middle of my glass house. I just recognize the consequences of being arrogant. Arrogance is not a lack of intelligence. Arrogance is jumping to judgment or drawing a conclusion without all the facts.

Then, because we have made our decision and judgments while ignoring the facts, we decide that something is wrong. Having done so, we are no longer open to see anything other than our judgment. We have put ourselves into a state contempt prior to investigation. And we choose to ignore all the other facts on the topic that may affect our opinion and/or judgment.

Think about a time when someone was arrogant with you. Or they said something hurtful when you made a mistake. Or you were just flat out wrong, and they decided that you were no more than that mistake. From that moment forward, they no longer listened, heard, understood, or saw you as anything else other than that mistake. How did that feel?

When suffering from arrogance, we use our intelligence to make judgments and decisions, and ignore every other fact that might support a different conclusion. When we do so, we really think we have something figured out. Then we stop learning about the person, place, or thing because we decided we know all that we need to know. The person, or thing that we've judged, continues to grow and change and passes us by. And in truth we no longer know anything about that.

Wouldn't it be better to form opinions about people's mistakes based on all the available information? Shouldn't we then allow them — even help them to grow past those mistakes? We should *love* them a little farther down the proper path — encouraging and strengthening them to be more than they currently are. The last question of about arrogance is this: when you make mistakes — and you will, how do you want to be treated?

Trap Seven: Wrath

Figure 7: The Heart of Wrath

The concept of wrath has often been misunderstood, both biblically, and otherwise. People believe that the sin of wrath means anger. But that's not true. Then what is wrath? The short answer — the real definition of wrath is *war*. When somebody has done us wrong, we get angry about it. That's an appropriate response. When we take justice into our own hands and seek to exact revenge, the resultant action is wrath. We literally go to war. You're out to pay them back. But payback costs — YOU.

Ask yourself this question. Has the cost of you going to war with people, places, or things been worth it? I'm not saying you should not stand up for yourself. I'm not saying you shouldn't defend your positions. I'm saying you should merely separate yourself from people who seek to do you damage. Rob me once shame on you. Rob me twice shame on me.

And who profits from war? Divorce is big business. More often than not, the process is drug out over time, and the only people that prosper are the lawyers and the divorce court system. The divorcees themselves pay dearly for their war. And, so do their children. Gee, they might all have to take out loans to maintain their lifestyles. Might the banks be bankrolling entertainment that espouses instant gratification in the form of casual sex and adultery? I wonder.

Look at our current political system, where two major parties are at constant war with one another. One group of constituents at war with another. We are truly a divided nation. The cost of these conflicts is in the trillions of dollars. Those trillions of dollars were sucked out of families when they go into debt over their wrath. Our economic system is supported by debt. Debt is amplified by wrath. We — all of us, are encouraged to impose our will in the form of wrath. It's the American way. Economies boom in times of war — even interpersonal wars.

We, being wrathful, need to separate ourselves from the anger. Anger is the appropriate response to an unjust situation. If anger is a result of injustice, then the way to quell our anger is justice. Justice is one of the seven cardinal virtues.

A cardinal virtue, by definition, is a personal behavior which is in strict accord with current moral, legal, and ethical guidelines of a certain place, or time. The interesting thing about that definition is the *personal behavior*. Justice is not something dispensed from a bench, or given to you by police, government, churches, friends or relatives. Justice is something you are — or are not. If you want *justice*, you must *be just*.

Model the behavior you want other people to treat *you* with. Treat people the way you want to be treated. Justice is *not* forgiving and allowing the other party to continue to damage you. Justice *is* akin to mercy. It is simply giving up your right to revenge, while shutting down their ability to do more damage. Take the lessons you've learned and move on in forgiveness of the offending party. And when I say forgiveness, I mean simply giving up your right to revenge and turning them over to the greater good.

CHAPTER 7: KEEPING UP WITH THE JONESES

If justice is a personal behavior in strict accord with current moral, ethical, and legal guidelines of a certain 'time or place; our 'time or place' gives us the ability to measure whether our own behaviors, or somebody else's, are in fact just. For instance, just because something is legal doesn't make it moral, or ethical.

Therefore, in my humble estimation, one of the biggest injustices in contemporary America are real estate loans based on one's ability to pay 60% percent of their income towards a mortgage. Just because it's legal to allow them to contractually allocate 60% of their income to a home mortgage doesn't make it moral or ethical. Leaving someone with only 40% of their income for all other needs, including property tax and homeowners' insurance is unjust. For they are sure to take on more debt to stay afloat.

30 years ago, home loan institutions allowed no more than 30% of somebody's income to go towards the mortgage. When they held that line, people had extra money to spend on restaurants, cars, appliances, furniture, movies and so on. Thus, leading to our wonderful capitalistic society being able to support itself through sales tax. This is the way America operated for 450 years.

Keeping down the cost of real estate led to long-term stable growth in the region and prosperity for everybody. But with the advent of television — and television commercials, Americans were cajoled into materialism. Having the newly advertised car became a status symbol, and a point of envy. And every other gadget became a point in a new game called "keeping up with the Joneses."

Allow me to begin with a paraphrased plagiarization of the 1968 ditty "Keeping up with the Joneses," written by Motown writing team Barret and Strong

"People gather round me. This is to whom it may concern. I'm not trying to run your life, but you're never too old to learn. Stop worrying about your neighbors, and the fancy things they've got. Because if you do, you'll find it's true, you're gonna wind up on the spot. Don't let the Joneses get you down.

"You may not believe it. But nine times out of ten it's true. The people you're trying to keep up with, are trying to keep up too. Remember that old saying; all that glitters ain't gold. Take heed, don't ignore it, and to your money tightly hold. Don't let the Joneses get you down.

"You're a leader yourself, but you don't even know it. You're so busy following the Joneses, you ain't got time to show it. Keeping up with the Joneses will only makes your life a mess. Bill collectors, tranquilizers, and getting deeper in debt. You better leave the Joneses alone.

"The Joneses got a new car today. Here's what you should say; hooray for the Joneses. Instead, you worry until your whole head turns gray — worrying about the Joneses. Just remember it's their car and they're the ones who had to pay. So, leave the Joneses alone. Listen, your car might be old. But remember — It never fails to get you where you want to go. You're doing fine. Don't let the Joneses blow your mind.

"Now listen. If you see something you want, and you know you can't afford it, then the very next thing for you to do is start saving towards it. The Joneses have been the downfall of many people you see. So, people, take my advice and let the Joneses be."

As the war of materialism escalates, so do prices. And when the venture capitalistic sharks get in the game, it gets worse and worse for the live-in homebuyer. I'm going to use my home city of Corona, California as an example. The following statistics are taken from the census' of 1990 and 2015. They have changed a little bit since 2015, but they will not be conclusive until the next census. The results are also augmented through other sources.

In 1990, the Corona, California median household income was about $98,000. There were 2.2 wage earners in the average home, combining their incomes, to earn that $98,000. The individual per capita income — from people working at McDonald's, all the way up, was $29,400. The average cost of a home in Corona California was $278,000. People were well able to afford their homes, their savings, and anything else.

Since then, real estate prices have skyrocketed. The current average home price in Corona is around $480,000. In the 2015 census, the individual income in Corona California had dropped to $28,000. Where real estate prices have almost doubled, the individual incomes have gone down. Household income for Corona, California has gone from $98,000 down to $89,000, since 1990. It now takes 3.4 wage earners to pay for the same house. Is this just?

The last paragraph does not even take into account the inflationary index on food, gas, water, and electricity. They've also doubled in the same period of time. The poverty level in Corona has increased by 46%. Going from 8.2% in 1990, to 12% in 2015. Again, I ask you, is this just? Are we being just — to our families, when we bite off more that we can chew?

Imagine a society of people focused on personal behaviors that are moral and ethical. In order for a behavior to be legal, it has to align with the letter of the law. Slavery was legal in America for centuries. But was it just? Would it be just if the racial tables were turned? Just because something is legal, if it's not moral and ethical, people should refrain from those behaviors. What would our society look like then? Would that not deescalate interpersonal wrath? Wrath and anger are incited when injustice is put upon somebody by your behaviors.

Trap Eight: Sloth

Figure 8: Slothful Existence

Many people get this one wrong. They confuse it with a different word — lazy. Sloth is a much more serious offense than just being lazy. Every now and again I feel lazy and don't follow through on something that I probably should have. That doesn't make me slothful. That just makes me human.

Sloth, by definition, is spiritual apathy. It is a giving up on the ideas and principles that make for an exciting and enthusiastic life. When your goals and dreams have died, life seems like an uphill battle. We just give up and say; why bother? Nothing that I do or say will matter anyway. So, I'm just going to stay here in my little comfortable bubble — unhappy but safe. Sloth enters into the money game very subtly.

This is another one that I struggled with myself. A lot of people subsist on a minimalistic lifestyle. They managed to step out of their shell a few times but retreated when they got overwhelmed. They are resolved to accept the condition of hopelessness. When you are engaged in a slothful lifestyle you cease trying to improve your position in life.

Commercialized loan companies have you living check to check with no savings. When emergencies arise, you have to use credit. Then the debt trap has you in its clutches. People who cherish credit ahead of savings or cash flow are dependent upon it. Imagine being able to pay cash for emergencies. If you had cash, you would not need the parasites, that need *you*, for their profit. Keeping you in debt is the only way they can profit. Thus, the culture and commercials push you to feel good now, and to heck with the consequences. The leaches have made us think we need them.

Someone who is slothful has traded their happiness and joy for comfort and conformity. Kahlil Gibran, in his book "The Prophet," put it like this: "for who among us likes to leave the walls of our pain, for it is familiar." In my work, I have seen hundreds of people with this affliction. The first step in defeating sloth is to understand the options that are available to you. It takes work to improve your situation.

If you have a job that is providing you a minimalist lifestyle, there is little hope for advancement. Look at the employees at your company that have been there five or 10 years longer than you. Are they happy? Is that who you want to be in five or 10 years? Do you want to be happy?

The cure to sloth is action. You'll never ever be able to feel your way into better actions. You have to act your way into better feelings. How many times have you said; I'll do it when I feel like it, even though it would be best for you to do it right now? I'm doing it with this book, right now.

My publisher is excited about getting this information out to the general public. I have to make a conscious decision on a daily basis to get up and write. I don't make excuses, like I don't have time, or I'm too busy, or whatever other horse crap I could come up with. I could easily be sidetracked in useless pursuits, like watching TV, or playing video games. And every now and then, I do. And then there's the dreaded Facebook rabbit hole.

But I know that at the end of the day, if I engage my slothful ways, I run the risk of failure. Here's what I also know. If I get up that day and I do the things that I said I was going to do — those things I've decided to do, to better my situation in my life, I feel better. I am more excited, and hopeful, at the end of the day than I was at the beginning.

The cure for sloth is the virtue 'fortitude'. Fortitude, in a nutshell, is doing the right thing — what you said you're going to do, despite how you feel at that time. How many times have you not followed through on something you said you're going to do? You felt okay for a minute, but how often does it sit right with you?

The lack of fortitude is one of the leading causes of depression in our society. With the gaming culture, TV, and social media, sloth has become a very profitable industry. Add to that; alcohol, marijuana and recreational drugs, and you get a whole demographic addicted to sloth. So, the question is; how much does being a sloth cost?

How many times have you failed to follow through on something that would've improved your situation? Estimate on how much money you have lost from not following through. Now add that to the savings calculator and see how much closer it gets you to your goal.

To summarize, sloth is spiritual apathy — why bother if it doesn't matter. The answer to sloth is fortitude — following through on what you said you're going to do — when you said you're going to do it. You cannot think your way into better actions, or feelings. You have to act your way into better thinking and feeling. Now answer this question. Is what you've been doing achieving the lifestyle that you want to live?

Next question. What is the lifestyle you want to live? Do you want to travel? Do you want to have a house paid off? Do you, like me, just want to be able to spend quality time with the people you love? Do you want to have a new house? Do you want a new car? Do you want everybody in your family to be happy and healthy? Do you want to be a blessing to your family and friends? Do you want to be able to do whatever you want, whenever you want, without worrying about money? And the big one — is what you're doing now, *ever* going to help you accomplish those dreams? Or, are you just playing it safe?

Let's itemize some of the ways that sloth might be costing you money.

1) How much do you spend on cable TV, or streaming service?
2) How many hours do you watch TV or movies?
3) Do you pay for subscriptions to any computer or video games? If so, how much does that cost?
4) How many hours do you spend playing those games each day?
5) Instead of cooking and cleaning up your dishes, how many times do you eat out, or bring home take out? How much did that cost?

6) What is the cost of the time you waste?

Just for fun, add up the total amount of hours you watch TV or play video games weekly. Then multiply it by 4.333 to find out how many hours you spend monthly. Next, take that number and divide by two [if you are paid twice a month]. Then multiply it by the hourly rate on your job.

Later in this book, were going to give you a new set of tools. These tools will help you make better decisions, based on your hopes and dreams for yourself and your family. Remember, once you're educated, it's all about the choices you make. It's my job to educate you and give you those choices. And it is my sincerest desire to be able to walk with you, and stand with you, and fight the fight with you. I want to see you, and your family, on the other side — happy joyous and free. Financial freedom is the ability to make decisions based on your character and faith — not your wallet. Now let's get you there.

CHAPTER 8: HEALTH IS WEALTH

Trap Nine: Gluttony

Figure 9: Hungry Whimpie

Gluttony is the lack of ability to moderate eating or drinking. It happens when we neglect our bodies basic needs. We crave more than its needs, to get a momentary feel-good fix. The cost of gluttony is manifested in health issues. Gluttony is not just overeating, it's over drinking, over watching TV, overindulging in recreational drugs or alcohol. An overindulgence in anything that is digested internally to make us feel better is considered gluttony.

Multi-billion-dollar industries have arisen based solely on gluttony. People pay more for diet pills than gym memberships. They pay ridiculous amounts on self-help books to try to think their way out of gluttony. Doctors, pharmacies, and dietitians soak up even more of people's money. Do you think for one minute that it's really in *their* best interest to solve your gluttony problem?

As of this morning, I weigh exactly 200 pounds. I am five feet and ten inches tall. Back when I was working, raising kids, and supporting my loved ones, I was neglecting myself. At the end of the working day — after eating dinner, I'd sit and watch TV. I wanted to make myself feel better about my life. Then I'd get up and put something in my mouth to make me feel even better. That wasn't a very good choice. Exactly one year ago I stepped on the scale, and I weighed 242 pounds.

My doctor said I was one step away from type II diabetes. I had high levels of good cholesterol, and higher levels of bad cholesterol. If I continued with those choices, the medicines I would've had to take would cost hundreds of thousands of dollars in my remaining lifetime. Around that time. my pastor — who was once a very large man himself, gave a sermon on the cost of his gluttony. He gave some of the wisest advice I've ever heard on the topic.

Toby Montgomery said that if he was ever asked to write a book about how he lost weight and got back into good health, it would be a very short book. There would be a one-page introduction and then six words on each page after that. It would be the same six words, in every language known known to man — one page after the other. And those six words would be, "shut your mouth and start moving". Very simply, eat less, and move more.

My first step was to move my office up to the second story. I walk up and down two flights of stairs dozens of times a day. I cut my meal portions in half. And, my between-meal snacks are far healthier than the choices I made before.

In my work, I deal with people that have massive amounts of medical debt, racked up through the cost of their gluttony and sloth. We have to fix their credit by getting their medical debt removed. Medical debt can be removed from a credit report because it's a HIPPA violation to put it there. Then the balances can be negotiated. The excessive cost of medical care has bankrupted many in our culture.

The remedy for gluttony is prudence. Prudence, in short, is wisdom. Eliminating the lust to spend money on things you do not need is the fruit of wisdom. One must think in terms of long-term peace and stability, instead of short-term excitement. It's just good common sense.

Also, understand that a person that indulges in gluttony pays two to four times more for food and drink than someone who does not. That excess weight could also cost you twice as much in life and health insurance premiums. Gluttony tied with sloth leads people to eat fast food — junk. Or, to eat out more than they can afford to. A decent amount of food for each person in the home, when shopping prudently, would be about $200 to $300 a month per person. A family of four's food budget should be around $900 to $1200 a month.

Let's see where you fall on the scale — no pun intended. Let's see what you're spending on food, drink, and nonessential consumption. When I work with people, this may seem a little intimidating, because sometimes we pay in cash and don't keep the receipt. If you use debit or credit cards for everything, it should be easy. If you pay partially, or totally in cash, just estimate. Fill in the blanks below for your entire household:

Table 2: Monthly Budget

How much do you spend at restaurants per month? _____
How much do you spend on groceries per month? _____
How much do you spend at the snack store per month? _____
How much do you spend at coffee shops per month? _____
How much do you spend on weight related medical bills per month? _____
How much do you spend on alcohol and tobacco per month? _____
How much do you spend on pleasure drugs per month? _____

Total cost of consumption: _____

Add these up to see how much your current choices have affected your finances. Are you comfortable with the conclusion? Yes or no? _____

If you could shift some of those resources away from the food and drink to your savings calculator; how much quicker would you be a millionaire?

You have power to choose. In 30 years, you can have weight related diabetes, or you can have a house paid off. Which one do you want?

CHAPTER 9: ENOUGH IS ENOUGH

Trap Ten: Greed

Figure 10: Ebenezer Scrooge

Greed is an obsession with gaining more than you could ever need. In eons past, greed was considered a sickness. The ramifications of people's greed are devastating to themselves and everybody around them. In America today, greed has become the measure of success. I've heard it said that the problem isn't that we can feed the poor. But rather, we can never satisfy the parasitic-rich. Greed has many devastating consequences — some are very subtle.

Greed is not the precursor to the financial woes in most people's lives. At least not their own greed. I've never been greedy. I've stepped over money many times to help people. I believe that people are more valuable than money. I'll refer to the golden rule again. Love God before all others, and your neighbor, as yourself.

Resources were never intended to be hoarded, by the few that have all the money, for them to dictate to the masses what they should or shouldn't do. Nor for the parasitic-rich to impose their beliefs on others, tossing them out of their homes if they disagree. Sounds a little draconian, but isn't that what we have here today?

People that are obsessed with money find their only happiness in gaining more. They exclude the cost of the people around them. It is never *just business*. But that is the creed by which greedy people tend to their affairs.

Here's a story from my own life. I was 28 years old, young and healthy. I met a girl online and fell in love. Through a series of events I found out that she was the daughter of a Filipino billionaire tycoon. We wanted to go out on dates, but she was constantly surrounded by bodyguards. She was never free to go anywhere because her parents were worried about her being kidnapped and held for a ransom. And the *subtle* cost was that they never trusted anybody. They always thought people were after their money.

I pleaded with her. I told her that I loved her before I even knew she had money. Things went well for about six months. I tried to explain to her that *she* was more valuable than money. But her mother and father convinced her that I was poor White trash, and not worthy of her adoration. They worshipped their wealth, expensive homes, luxery cars, boats and vacations. Their greed had become the prison in which they lived. And they shackled their daughter in that same prison, even though she lived on the other side of the planet.

I took her and my young son to the park one day. She couldn't even play — she didn't know how. Her bodyguards turned the park into a three-person cellblock. In short order, the playdate was ended because of her bodyguards.

She was raised to trust no one. They surrounded her with paid servants and hirelings. As long as they were able to pay, she was comfortable. But she was never free. In the end I concluded that they preferred to live in a soft beautiful prison. But they were alone — totally unable to know what love was. They couldn't trust anybody who wasn't as greedy as they were. I got a firsthand look at the emotional devastation caused by greed. Many Filipinos live in abject poverty, while a few live-in opulent luxury.

Let's look at a super-wealthy American family, who for generations (because of greed) never allowed anybody to marry outside of their wealthy family. Inbreeding created a monster that ended up killing the United States wrestling team's coach on their property. And thus, ended the family dynasty. Their greed became a genetic prison, with devastating consequences for the community at-large.

I watched as greed ran rampant through the Southern California real estate industry. In 1993, I was able to buy my first real house with the help of a good friend. Real estate prices were very high, but optimism was great because people's incomes had gone up consistently with real estate prices.

In the mid-1990s the housing market hit the tipping point. Interest rates rose, and home prices crashed. Thousands of people who were in the real estate and mortgage industry lost their jobs. And thousands of people in our community lost their homes. Who did they lose their homes *to*? The banks and the banks' investors.

After watching that devastation, the real estate and mortgage professionals in the area swore that it would never happen again. They would never *let* it happen again. Who is *they*, I wondered? They were going to restrict the amount of money that people were paying for their homes to a standard 30% of their income. No more than 30% of people's income could go towards the housing.

Then came 2003, 2004 and 2005. And I watched while *'they'* make money by putting people in mortgages that were way above 30% of their income. It turns out that *'they'* were the foxes guarding the henhouse. *They* started selling more houses and making more money and becoming accustomed to the lifestyle. The measurement by which people would be able to afford their homes got skewed again. The foxes were adjusting POI (percentage of income) to feed their own greed. When POI hit 50%, housing prices skyrocketed.

But this time people's income had not gone up with home prices. In order for the foxes to sustain their own lifestyle, *they* agreed to compromise their values and cajole people into signing 'subprime' mortgages that far exceeded people's ability to pay. Then came the inevitable crash. The 'subprime' mortgage crisis. 'Upside-down' homeowners were forced to 'short-sell' their home for far less than what they owed on the loan. Short sales and foreclosures skyrocketed. People lost their homes and jobs, again. And one more time, the real estate industry says *they* will never let this happen again. *They* are the industry and government regulators. *They* are the foxes waiting for the next batch of eggs to hatch.

There are a few people, at the top of the food chain, who make their money off of real estate investing. Without naming names of corporations, like Goldman Sachs, I'll explain how the deck is stacked against the masses. They discovered that they could sell a house over and over again, binding a different family to an ever-increasing mortgage each time. Those people would fight — do everything they could to pay the inflated loan and keep their home for as long as they could. The homeowners don't realize that the game is rigged.

The loan is DESIGNED to make them default on the loan. The bank repossesses the house and the parasites wait for another deluded family to buy the same home. One home — sold multiple times. With high enough interest rates, they can sell the same home, every two or three years, collecting 30 years' worth of interest with every three-year cycle.

Knowing that the industry would eventually tank, because of their greed, they bought insurance policies to cover the losses. When the economy did in fact tank, the mortgage companies and bankers ended up getting paid by those insurance policies for their losses. Those properties then got transferred to a subsidiary bank, owned by the same corporations, and sold again for profit.

These people have no consideration for the good of our community as a whole. Greed has isolated them from the devastating effects deluged on the people around them. Greed has created a mindset that says it's okay to take advantage of people because they are uneducated as to the pitfalls of home buying. They do this all day — every day. You may only get to buy one home per generation. That's once every 20 years — to their all day, every day. At that rate, you won't catch on until you're no longer able to earn a living. *They* can suck away a person's entire life earnings, and still sleep at night.

Here's a question I have for the greedy. How much is enough? Personally, if I had 2.25 million invested wisely, I could live off the interest ($13,000 a month) without putting a dent in the 2.25 million. I could own a beautiful home, be able to save and invest money, and make sure that my family is happy and healthy. I could support my church and my community. All that, and still leave money for my children and grandchildren. That would be enough — for *me*.

However, it's not up to me to try to regulate what is enough for other people. The Bible is full of rich people who have done wonderful things. Being rich is not a sin. Being rich is not something to be abhorred. A wise person's wealth is an opportunity to bless others from an overflowing cup. Wealth can be a beautiful thing.

We will never be able to pass laws to regulate people *into* morality and wise decisions. Evil will still be evil, and greed will still be greed. But if we empower and educate people as to the ramifications of greed and put the focus on things that bring long-term peace and serenity, we just might have a chance to work our way out of this national calamity. The answer to greed is the virtue of 'charity'.

Charity is biblically synonymous with love. But love has become a washed-out word. Charity, by definition, is a spiritual love of others. If you have charity you view everybody as equal. Surely there would be no greater or lesser people than you, yourself. You will view everything that you receive as a blessing and you will endeavor to bless others. You will treat people as you would want to be treated. Thus, building a community of strong, happy, healthy people that you get to live and work with. Your day-to-day interpersonal relationships will thrive.

CHAPTER 10: REHUMANIZATION

Trap Eleven: Dehumanization

Figure 11: Human Devaluation

I want to paint a picture for you. A picture of a successful and well balanced *you*. This is the end goal of everything I'm doing. Our forefathers insisted that all men are created equal. What would happen if we *really* believed it? We would start adopting personal behaviors that are just. We would no longer hate people. We would no longer dehumanize entire populations.

To coax men into war, the enemy must first be dehumanized. I can't imagine the mindset it takes to destroy an innocent human life. Now portray that same soul as a rabid dog, and the entire community will hunt it down and kill it. This book is not just about financial balance. It's also about common decency. We must seek to rehumanize those we see around us. We must view their families' wellbeing as holding just as much value as our own. In essence, we all belong to one family — the human family. We are all members of the human race.

When I see mankind in this new light, the biblical standard of love shines through, and that darkness called fear is wiped out. Then, there is no need to hoard riches, as if riches are a means of protection. With that in mind it is perfectly reasonable to start a company that profits me — the owner just 10% of the revenue stream. Ten percent goes to me and my family, and ninety percent goes to providing for the needs of the people around me. Whether dealing in real estate, medical insurance, or education, my love is expressed as charity. And charity — true charity cannot exist unless all lives matter.

This corporation of mine focuses on teaching people the wisdom of virtue, and the foolishness of sin. And through this corporation, we systematically teach people how to get out of debt, stay out of debt, save money and live free. As personal savings grow — through virtuous living, we attack people's easy debt targets. Then we use the money saved by eliminating the low hanging fruit to attack harder targets. You will have a complete plan to eliminate parasitic debt by the time this course is completed.

You will establish a heathy nest egg as proof that you understand the wisdom of the principles we teach. We will help you develop your plan to be financially free in the process. And you will be in a position to educate your family and friends. We could go one city at a time, systematically paying off mortgages and credit card debt until no one is left in debt. We could go back to doing business with each other, rather than working for gas money, to get back to work. We could live at home rather than visiting our homes at night.

Imagine whole cities where human beings are free to go, and buy, or do whatever they want, whenever they want. The revenue to maintain roads and schools would be generated through the taxes on the sales that are made every day on our own goods and services. Those goods and services are produced by happy, healthy, secure people in their own communities. And love thy neighbor as thyself is the paradigm by which they operate. Imagine what that city would be like. And imagine what it would be like for greedy people to finally be free of the cushy prisons that they've created. They'd be re-humanized.

Trap Twelve: Lust

Figure 12: Peppy La Pew

Lust is this insatiable desire to have *more* of something that makes you feel good, even though *more* is unhealthy. This happens when people are emotionally unequipped to know that long-term intimacy, and true connection with the people around them, is far more beneficial than a transactional short-term high. People want connection. They want to feel loved and respected.

Our commercialized society exploits lust as a means to sell their products and services. They say that sex sells. And we buy what they're selling, because sex is an easy way to achieve that connection, we all crave. It's the only way that some of us know of to make ourselves feel good. Even if it's for just a minute of ecstasy, they crave it like crack cocaine.

But when real intimacy approaches, they have no idea what to do with it. They run away or blow it up. Just to repeat the cycle over and over, again and again. The idea of pursuing lust as a means for emotional security, is like trying to stay warm by lighting a pack of firecrackers. That excitement gives us warmth for a minute, leaving us injured and cold, afterwards. Since it's the only way we know to get warm, we go through long stretches of cold, seeking that excitement over and over again. What if you just learned how to build a fire and maintain it. It may take a little bit more work, in the beginning, but it provides a much more secure and stable source of well-being in the long run.

Lust has become a pseudo-virtue. People measure the quality of their relationships almost solely on the quantity and the quality of their sex lives. If people are overly concerned about sex, hurt feelings will surely arise. Instead of learning how to work and grow through those feelings, and become closer as a result, people become slaves to the drama of it all. And the drama produces more hurt feelings. Being a slave to the pain of romantic drama costs lots of money. Reread the chapter on divorce.

Many products and services are completely dependent upon the quality and quantity of your sex life? How many times have you bought something to make yourself feel sexy? Being sexy is cute; right? Sexy makes us feel attractive; right? So be as provocative as you possibly can. But what sort of people are you attracting? Who are you actually provoking? Most likely it's a person who is as broken and disconnected from the workings of a healthy family life as you are.

Just because someone finds you desirable does not mean they love you. They'll stick around as long as they can get more from you than they give. Hit a rough patch and they are out of here like last year. Oh look — there's another broken home. And more blood in the water for the loan . . . sharks.

The word love has been confused with lust. There are three perfectly acceptable standards of love, and all three are beneficial to the soul. But none of them, in excess, is healthy. In balance, they are very healthy. The first type is *Eros.* From Eros, we get the English word erotic. Eros is the physical attraction of love. It's the part that says this person turns me on. Without Eros, we would have no future generations. But that is where most people stop.

Excessive lust retards the growth of a healthy relationship. In the course of relationships, there are ups and downs. If love is simply based on fickle feelings that come and go like the wind, the relationship will not last past the fireworks.

The second part of love is *Philia* — as in Philadelphia, the city of brotherly love. This is the love that you have for somebody based on who they are. You like them. They make you feel good. You like them the way there are. They are there for you, and you're there for them. In modern vernacular, you're *besties.*

There is a problem with stopping at Philia. People change and grow. And the feelings that they bring out in you ebb and flow. Someone that was once dear to you may end up not being so dear after a while. This is the nature of all relationships. So, if your love is based solely on the way that somebody makes you feel, then your relationships are doomed from the beginning.

Having Philia love is important, but if it is the only measure of love, you will end up spending a lot of time lost and alone. People will eventually hurt your feelings. That is the true nature of relationships. People will hurt you, but they will also help you and make you better. They will also change. The feelings that were once there will dissipate.

Then comes the last level of love — *Agape.* This is love that's based not on who you are, but on who you decided to be. It is the love that continues despite the feelings. The best example I have in my love life, is the love that I have for my children. I love them because I've decided to. I love them because I choose to, no matter how they make me feel. And Lord knows they don't always make me feel good. The result of this decision has had awesome affects. Long-term and lasting effects. And yes, I've chosen to endure the momentary sufferings of change, and still love these people.

Agape without *Eros* and *Philia* is not wise either. You can love somebody *and* not allow them to hurt you. Love doesn't mean you accept all their faults and defects. Agape love does not mean that you become a doormat. Agape means that I have to learn how to effectively communicate, in a loving way, during difficult times. I have to choose to work through those times. And sometimes I have to love somebody from afar because they make choices that are hurtful to me. But in the end, having Agape love gives the longest lasting and best sense of peace and security.

Agape is the way that I believe God chooses to love me, despite my thoughts and sometimes my very ill choices. God has always come through. Despite my arguments, rejection, bitterness, sadness and anger, God did not leave me. And He loved me enough to let me go my way, until I came back and humbly asked for forgiveness and guidance. If you're looking for an example of Agape love, all you have to do is read the story of Jesus Christ. He is the *best* example.

Jesus Christ was bold in His love and forgiveness. Christianity is not just opening up the Bible and reading what Christ did and said. In Christ you will find the only person that truly models the behavior that you should seek to emulate.

Lust is defect of character that is sure to cost you plenty. Answer the following questions, if you dare.

Do you know what real intimacy is? _____
Do you know the benefits of having a long-term loving relationship? _____
How much has pursuing sexual gratification over intimacy cost you? _____
If you put that money in the savings calculator at 6 ½% interest, how much would you have available in your bank account now? _____

Trap Thirteen: Envy

Figure 13: The Faces of Envy

Here's how envy manifests itself:

"How can that person have so much, when they are less deserving of it than me? Why can't I be cool like them?"

Are they less of a person than you are? Are they less *human* than you? Envy manifests in one's life because they are constantly judging their insides by everybody else's outsides. The envious are ego maniacs with inferiority complexes.

"Those people have these things and they seem happy, so if I had those things, I would be happy too."

The problem with that spirit is that happiness is not contingent upon what you do, or do not have. Happiness is contingent upon a decision to be happy. True happiness is learning to appreciate what you have, instead of constantly seeking what you don't have.

You can see this in people's lives when they're constantly saying, "if I just had that new house. Or if I just had that new car. Or if I just had the right job. Or if I just had the right help. Or if I just had that successful person's charisma. Or if I had just been born on the right side of the tracks."

And so on, and so on. Always looking for something, or somebody to fix the way they feel inside.

I live in a three-bedroom townhouse. It's in a great neighborhood. It has a little bit higher rent than I wanted to pay, but it suits my needs for home and office just fine. I've been able to live here for the last 13 years and God has blessed me with the ability to uphold and maintain my lifestyle. But then my ego starts looking at the way other people live. People who seem happier than me. So now my mind will start focusing on how to get those things that appear to make other people happy.

Long ago, I chose to be happy with this home. I chose to accept that this is where God has wanted me to be. This is where I will grow and prosper. Other people may look happy on the outside, but I have no idea what's going on inside them. I cannot judge my insides based on their outsides. I can either be happy with my own circumstances, or I can constantly be looking for something else, somewhere else.

I was once getting off the plane at an airport. I was on my way home. And as I was coming down the escalator to the baggage claim, I noticed a small family — a mother, a baby and little girl standing expectantly at the bottom of the escalator. It was clear to me that they were waiting for someone. As I got my bags, I heard the little girl screaming with excitement. I turned around just in time to see her run over and jump into her daddy's arms. The whole family was happy to see him. It was a tearjerker of a happy scene.

As I went out to the curb to wait for a taxi, the family came up next to me. As they were waiting for the crosswalk light to change, the father took a knee and looked his little girl in the eyes.

"I love you so much," he told her. "I'm sorry I missed your recital. I heard all about it, But I want to hear about it all from *you*. I can't wait to spend time with you and get caught up."

The little girl spun in a circle and giggled. The man stood up and took the baby from the mother's arms. He pushed the baby up in the air and gave him a little shake. The baby laughed, and the man pulled him into his chest.

"I love you too," The father cooed. "I'm so happy to see you. I can't wait to spend more time with you. You're almost ready to walk."

The man seemed very happy to be home.

Then he put the baby in the little girl's arms and turned to his wife. He smiled, and she smiled back at him. Without any words, they walked up to each other and embraced. They held each other for what seemed like an eternity, but it was really only about 30 seconds. When they broke the embrace, they looked each other in the eyes, and gave each other a passionate kiss on the lips, like no one else was around.

Then he smiled.

"I really missed you," he told his wife. "I am just so looking forward to spending time with you. I am so happy to see you. I can hardly wait to get caught up on everybody — the kids, and the neighbors, and the family. And I just missed you *so* much."

His wife was in tears.

"I miss you too honey. I can't wait to hear about your work, and all the things that you've accomplished. We are blessed to have you in our lives. I'm so happy to see you too."

I reached over and tapped the man on the shoulder.

"Yes, can I help you," he asked.

And I said, "listen, I just want to know why you guys are so happy. I mean what happened? How did you get to be so happy? I just really love seeing you and your family like this."

He cocked his head and he looked at me.

"'Cause, man, it's not something that happened to me. it's something I decided."

How much money have you spent chasing the right things, or people, or places to make yourself feel better? How much time have you wasted being unhappy — not looking at the blessings that you have? How much money has envy cost you? How many things have you bought, that you really didn't need, in the pursuit of happiness?

Here's a story about a young man who entered the military. He went through his career and progressed up the ranks. At the end of his career, he had all the money he needed for retirement. His family never lacked for anything. At his retirement ceremony he stood up and gave a speech. He, being known and loved by many, was asked to explain how he was able to be so successful in his personal life. And he told his secret.

"When I was a lieutenant, I spent money like I was a private. When I was a captain, I spent money like I was a private. When I made major, *we* spent money like I was a private. When I finally made colonel, we spent money like I was a lieutenant. I was never discontent with my home. We never spent more than we budgeted. We saved a bunch of money, and now I get to do anything I want for the rest of my life. And, so does my family."

THE DEBT TRAP — JOHN CHAMPION

This retired colonel amassed a fortune through gratitude and discipline. He lived on a mountain of savings, rather than in a valley of debt and despair. He never dug a hole in the first place. So, he never had to dig his way out.

CHAPTER 11: OTHER ECONOMIC FACTORS

Trap Fourteen: Inflation

Figure 14: The Silent Predator

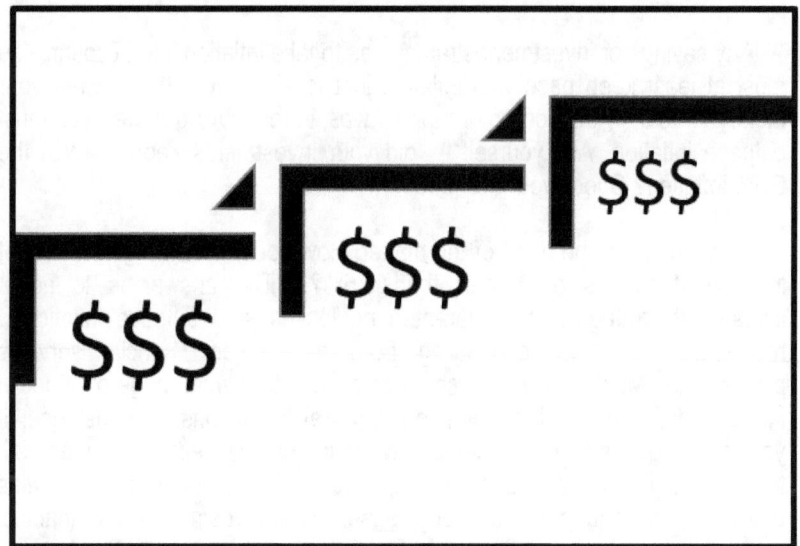

Many people that I counsel do not take into account the cost of inflation in their savings and budgeting strategies. Inflation is a constant drain on your money and your prosperity. It can subtly sneak in and wipe away your future, if you are not paying attention.

Depending on who you listen to, inflation over the last 15 years has averaged anywhere between 3.5% and 6% a year. Let's call it 4%. Any savings or investment strategy that earns you less than 4% means that your money is worth less at the end of the year than it was at the beginning. If, at the beginning of the year you had $10,000 in your bank account growing at 1% (more than likely it's less) interest — at the end of the year you would have $10,100. If inflation was 4%, then the purchasing power of that $10,100 is actually $9700.

The inflation indexes vary so much, because different entities use different metrics to paint whatever image they want. For instance, in the federal government's inflation index, they exclude things like food, gas, electricity — things that have significantly increased over the last 15 or 20 years. But if you look at real estate over the last 20 years, while the prices have gone up and down like a roller-coaster, overall prices have only gone up about 2% to 3%. Taking all of that into consideration, the inflation index is probably more like 5.5%.

Any savings or investment strategy has to take inflation into account. You must at least keep pace with inflation just to stay even. If you want your money to actually be worth more *than it was*, in real buying power, you must outpace inflation. Ask yourself — did your investments keep up with the 5.5% inflation? Check your accounts.

Now we are at the heart of the matter. How does the average citizen get investment returns of greater than 5.5%? The answer is to adopt investment strategies that guarantee no losses, and outpace inflation. I recommend you get counseling from a licensed financial services professional. Make sure he, or she, has access to a wide range of financial instruments, from a wide range on financial institutions. For instance, if you're talking to somebody that is only insurance licensed, they cannot talk to you about any product that can generate a loss. Those are securities products, that require a securities license. Stock investments and financial advice also require special licenses. The following chart may be helpful.

Figure 15: Financial Services Licenses

Exam	License Type	Type of Compensation	Purpose
Series 7	Broker/Dealer (RR)	Commissions for transactions	General Securities
Series 6	Broker/Dealer (RR)	Commissions for transactions	Packaged Products
Series 63	Broker/Dealer (RR)	Commissions for transactions	State Law Reciprocity
Series 65	Investment Advisor Rep (IAR)	Fee for service	Investment Management
Series 66	Investment Advisor Rep (IAR)	Fee for service	Combines Series 63 and 65 exams

The rules prohibit people that are not licensed, like financial entertainers, from talking about products and services that require licenses. Not only will you not get competent advice — it's illegal. People that are not fully licensed, will only try to sell you the products or services that they are licensed to sell. You want someone that has full access to the full range of products, so they can make a competent plan for you. Every savings and investment plan should be tailored specifically to you. We'll get into the details of competent financial planning later in this book.

Trap Fifteen: Income Stagnation

Stagnation is another silent killer. The following figure shows the income growth for males and females in the United States, since 1971, in comparison to the cost of the college education in 1971. In a dollar for dollar comparison women's income went up marginally, since 1971, while men's income has gone down. It is very difficult to save money and get ahead when your wages have stagnated.

Figure 16: The True Cost of College

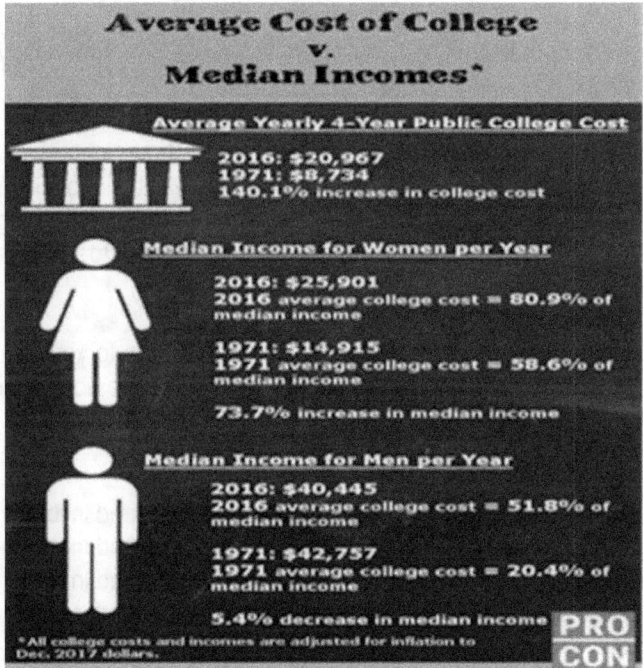

But what can be done about it, when men's income is lower than they were almost 50 years ago, and women still earn less than men? Basic math tells us that it takes at least two incomes to even come close to match the rate of inflation. To actually outpace inflation, it takes more than two income streams per family.

What opportunities do you have available to you to make extra money? You are working as hard as you can, and money is still going out the door as fast as it's coming in. If you don't seem to have any answers, you'd better keep reading.

The good news is that we live in an extremely entrepreneurial society. Everybody has the ability to develop multiple income streams. You could take on a second job, essentially trading your remaining waking hours for money. But your time is only worth what people tell you it is worth.

Or, you can look into starting businesses of your own. There are thousands of small businesses that you can start with little, or no money. I used to shovel snow out of peoples' driveways, so they could drive to work. And guess what; they paid whatever I asked. You get to decide what you're worth. Is what you're doing currently working? Will continuing to do that, and adding more of the same, get you where you need to be? Are you willing to try something new and step out of your comfort zone?

That's right, I said comfort zone. Many people trade immediate comfort for happiness. They are not happy, but comfortable in their condition. You're either going to continue to work to make somebody else's dreams come true at the expense of your dreams, or you're going to work to make your own dreams come true.

I want you to list the business opportunities available to you, below. This is a brain-storming exercise, so don't hold back. There are no bad ideas.

Table 3: Opportunity Costs

Opportunity 1: _____ Startup cost _____ Desired income _____
Opportunity 2: _____ Startup cost _____ Desired income _____
Opportunity 3: _____ Startup cost _____ Desired income _____
Opportunity 4: _____ Startup cost _____ Desired income _____
Opportunity 5: _____ Startup cost _____ Desired income _____
Opportunity 6: _____ Startup cost _____ Desired income _____

You might need to extend a little income out now, but without *any* risk there can be no reward. More risk — more reward. You may fail one or two times before you find the thing that actually takes off. Keep going until you succeed. You never know which seed God will bless. Never ever give up on your hopes and dreams. As you consider the options you listed, I want you to look back over your life and think about what's fun — to you. If you do what makes you happy, it's not work. Now figure out which opportunity best suits *you*. You will find that when you love what you are doing, the money will come easy. Have the faith to step into your true calling.

Trap Sixteen. Lack of Planning

Figure 17: Failing to Plan

I've heard it said that people don't plan to fail — they fail to plan. And I do agree with that. My gripe is that people have not been taught how to plan, or how to follow through on those plans. We have been conditioned to follow orders and to do as we're told, trusting that other people's plans will bring about success in our own lives. But what if the people you're trusting don't care about your success? After years on the same job, with a string of fifty cent raises, it should be obvious that your well-being is not part of their plan. Why not come up with your own plan for success. There are six fundamentals in any sound financial plan

1) **Cash flow:** this is an objective look at what's coming in *and* what's going out of your family economy. Look at where every nickel goes, and where it comes from.
2) **Emergency fund:** decide how much you need to have in liquid assets — cash to cover your basic living expenses for six months to a year. Objectively, create that target and devise a plan to get there. Remember money in the bank (liquid assets) is the key to living free.
3) **Debt management:** have a systematic plan that puts leverage in your favor — collecting interest rather than paying interest. This action will get you out of debt, completely, as quickly as possible. Thus, freeing up lots of capital for the next step.
4) **Asset protection:** insurance against loss. If there is a loss to income, or material goods, our home and family should be indemnified, or be restored to its previous status as best as possible. This should be a huge priority. Insurance makes a poor man rich. Odds are that you have auto insurance. Surely your life is of far greater value than your car. Do you have life insurance? Insurance costs less, in most cases, than the money you waste on bad habits.

I talk to a lot of people who say they are broke. They tell me they don't have any extra money to protect their family. In many cases it's just a matter of choices. A friend of mine who is married with two young children, has been talking about starting a life insurance policy for himself. He assumes that $500,000 will take care of his wife and kids, in the event of his untimely demise. The premium for a 30-year policy would be around $48 a month, because he's young and healthy. He's complaining that with all the bills, he doesn't that have much left over. He says he needs the Sunday football NFL ticket. He says his wife and kids are his priority, but in reality, the Dallas Cowboys are.

Then the same man who was too broke to spend $48 to protect his family went out and bought a new car and put vanity plates on the car. Those vanity plates cost about the price of life insurance for the year. And if anything happens to him, his wife and children are left with nothing but his debts. The car will be repossessed — vanity plates and all.

5) **Asset accumulation:** Now that you have a better understanding of some of the challenges in building a family fortune, this should be easier to understand. You should be able to save money, earn an interest rate that outpaces inflation, protect the principle, and get tax advantages on distribution.

This doesn't just happen by chance. This happens by choice. And rarely will this ever happen when you take advice from your broke cousin instead of a competent financial professional. Don't be unwise. Seek a licensed professional that is under obligation, by law, to do what's best for you and your family.

6) **Asset distribution:** if you don't specify who gets your assets, should something happen to you, the government will step in and decide for you. If your case goes to probate, your family could lose up to half of your investments to estate taxes. If you don't leave instructions for the placement for your minor children, the state will decide where they go, and what kind of resources they will have when they get there.

You must have both a solid *will*, and in most cases a *trust*, to make sure that your wishes are honored. When it comes time to distribute your assets, the government is first in line, the lawyers are second in line, and your family is *last* in line. You can easily cut the lawyers and the government out, and just leave it all for your family.

CHAPTER 12: CRITICAL THINKING

One of the most impactful books that I've ever read was "Brain Power," by Karl Albrecht. Mr. Albrecht wrote this book with hopes that it would become a college level course on how to use your brain to its greatest potential. In summary, your brain is the most powerful supercomputer ever devised. But if not understood properly, it can be easily deceived. So, how do you decide what is true or not a true?

Mr. Albrecht accurately concluded that we live in a society that pushes people to make emotionally based decisions. He said that making long-term decisions based on short-term feelings was foolhardy. Furthermore, some people have abandoned the pursuit of truth altogether, because somebody said something out of passion that turned out not to be true. These days we call it *fake news*. If you can't trust the news, why bother believing anybody?

Often, when we make these emotional conclusions, we shut down any constructive communication on the topic. Once we've decided we know what's true, and passed judgement on an issue or situation, we are no longer open to receiving any more information on the topic. The situation can — and probably *will* change, but our judgment stays the same. At that point we are unable to see the truth about the matter at all.

What is a truth? The definition is far more interesting than I thought it would be. The simplistic definition is; a fact that is preceded and justified with conclusive evidence related to an individual, entity, ideology, or geographic region. In essence, truth is something that can be proved.

Just because somebody makes an impassioned statement, doesn't make it true. They must have documented verifiable evidence of that statement. We have seen many supposed leaders and authorities say that something is a fact just because somebody else said it — with no proof at all. We have heard them state that their proof was simply that somebody *said*, that somebody else *said*, something without offering any real evidence.

This path to deception and manipulation could lead us to civil war. If we don't challenge ourselves to learn how to draw conclusions based on evidence, and unite under those basic truths, the truth cannot set us free. If we examine the evidence to determine the truth, and accept whatever truth that the evidence proves, then we can unite and fix many things. Only then will the truth set us free.

At the risk of becoming controversial, I want to take on the theory of evolution. Charles Darwin was sailing around remote islands when he noticed that the birds he saw there were different than the birds he saw anywhere else. What he saw was the evolutionary *fact* of microevolution. Microevolution is the part of the theory of evolution that nobody argues with. Microevolution is the observation that species adapt to their environment. Not only do they adapt to their environment, the species adapt to the ecological and social conditions to which they are exposed.

So, let's all agree that regardless of religion, or ideology, that the fact of microevolution is absolutely true. How do we know it's a truth? We know it because it has passed the test of the scientific method.

The scientific method is what the scientific community deems the process by which something can be scientifically called a truth. It essentially states that:

1) You must have a theory.
2) You must be able to observe it.
3) You must be able to measure it.
4) You must be able to reproduce it in a controlled environment.

And If you can do all of those things, then the theory can be called a scientific fact. Microevolution passes these proofs. The problem arises when the rest of the theory is forced on us as fact.

The first assumption in the theory of evolution, as it's taught in schools, states that there was a big bang. And from that Big Bang, *nothing* brought forth *something*. In essence, there was nothing, and then there was something. In order to call that a fact, we would have to be able to observe, measure, and reproduce the process — bringing forth something, from nothing, in a controlled environment.

While still seeking evidence of this *pseudo*-truth, our children are taught the theory of evolution as if it were a fact. There has never been any scientist who could remotely prove that something could come from nothing. It is a scientific impossibility.

With all of modern science, man can't even recreate the nothingness, that the something came from. For, nothingness is not merely an empty space — it's not even outer space. The nothingness referred to in the Big Bang theory is the absence of space itself. It means non-existence. We can't even take the first step in the theory because man is not capable of uncreating anything. Split an atom, and you still have the subatomic particles.

Unfortunately, that is not where the theory of evolution stops. According to the theory, the Big Bang created a bunch of inanimate objects, rocks, flying randomly through space. Then the theory gets really tricky with the concept of abiogenesis. Abiogenesis is the part of the theory that says that inanimate objects somehow became animate. That dead lifeless material somehow became living. That this flying rock we call Earth somehow magically self-generated living material. This is a part of the theory that has been *disproven* by scientists over, and over again. Not one time, to this date, has a scientist ever been able to take inanimate material, and make it come alive. Since abiogenesis does not pass the scientific method, why is that being taught as scientific truth?

The next part of the theory of evolution is macro evolution. That is the theory that one species turned into another species. That man came from apes. Fossil records have shown that the bones of apes and the bones of men are different sizes and shapes. Anthropologists have never found the missing link, that proves that we came from apes, in the fossil record. Not one time has a middle-species fossil been found. There's never been a fossil that shows that, somehow, horses came from dogs. There's never been a fossil that shows that alligators turned into birds.

Despite looking for over 150 years, we have not been able to observe, reproduce, or measure results that prove macro evolution. It would be like me making the statement that Spiderman was real, based on the fact that there are spiders and there are men. With no proof — only conjecture, evolution is taught in schools as if it were a scientific fact. And further, that all life evolved from some primordial slime, or single celled life form akin to an amoeba. And that amoeba somehow morphed into plant life and became the basis for *all* animal life. And that primordial plant life became mold that turned into seaweed, trees, flowers, wheat, corn, barley, apples, pears, and so forth.

They assume — and teach that amoebas turned into tadpoles, fish, crawling fish, air breathing crawling fish, dinosaurs, birds, mammals, dogs, cats, Neanderthals, apes and man. And that the whole random chain of events somehow resulted with you sitting here today reading this book.

Does any of that pass the scientific method? The answer is no. And yet we have it shoved down our throats as scientific fact. You don't need a scientific reason to reject the idea of a master architect. Everyone is free to believe that every house on earth built itself by accident.

Once we start investigating what is true, we have to accept that we have a limited experience on most topics. I grew up in Nebraska. In Nebraska it would be a conclusive statement of a fact to say there are lots of tornadoes. That would be the truth, even if somebody that grew up in California never witnessed lots of tornado. It would be true — in California to say that tornadoes hardly ever happened, but earthquakes happen all the time. But the truth — in Nebraska is that earthquakes don't happen that often at all.

Both are conflicting statements, but both our truths. If you are sincere about pursuing truth. you must be open to all information regarding the topic. You should also be open to the fact that another person's experience sometimes trumps *your* truth. And if we can apply this method to the discernment of truth, then we stand a chance at being able to unite under a truth. We could have *real* justice in this world.

So back to Mr. Albrecht's book brainpower. The brain is divided into two sides — or hemispheres. We have a left brain and right brain. The left brain is the fact-finding logical side, and the right brain is the creative, interpretive, emotional side. His conclusion was that both sides — emotional and intellectual hold equal value. However, some people are more *left-brained*, while others are more *right-brained*. And the differences bring balance to our society.

When both the emotional and the intellectual combine to make decisions, those decisions tend to be better for ourselves and for our communities as a whole. Intellect without empathy is as devoid of wisdom, as empathy without intellect.

Hemispheres aside, there are four levels of consciousness. Each of those levels of consciousness have critical functions. And each can be scientifically measured by the frequency that the brain emits while in that functional state. We've all heard of brain waves; right? They can be measured using a medical device called an electroencephalogram (EEG.)

Figure 18: Brainwaves

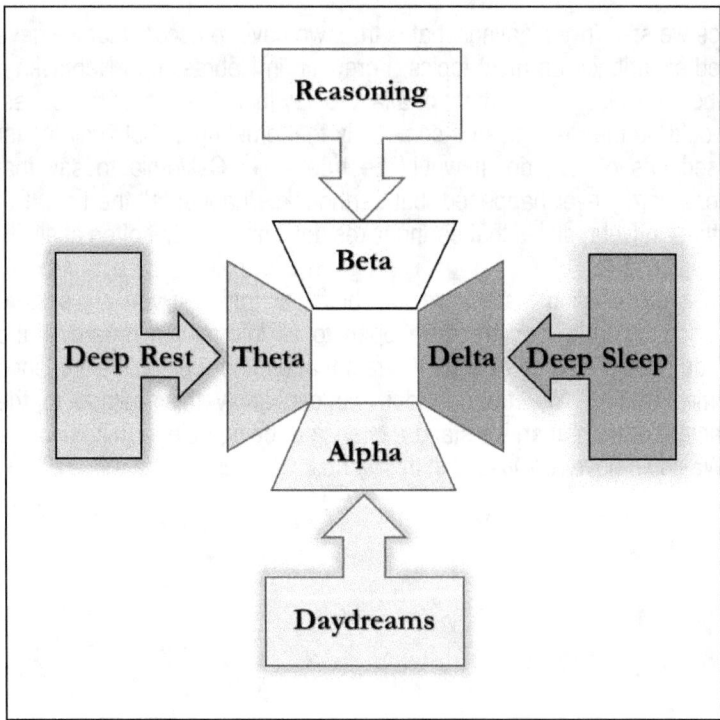

The first level of our brain deals with reasoning. Beta-waves manifest when our brain processes what we see, hear, think, and feel — *right now*. In the Beta state, our brain is a real-time sensory processor. At this level, the brain is very simplistic. Our response is a judgement — good or bad, right or wrong, pain or pleasure? We are deciding if something is worth expending time and energy, or not? Is it dangerous or beneficial? Should I fight or flee? This level of the brain brings to bare our core instincts, while observing our immediate surroundings and circumstances.

The next level of consciousness is the Alpha state. In this state, our brain compares our current circumstances with past situations. We, in a sense, *daydream* through our historical records. We do so because we have found the situation non-threatening and possibly beneficial. So, we have time to muse over the possibilities. The EEG would show Alpha waves while we are in this state. To those around us we would appear to be distracted to the point of being *somewhere else*.

The Beta and Alpha assessments decide if the circumstance is an opportunity or a threat, and then whether or not it will be beneficial in the short-term, and — or long-term. Compulsive individuals tend to give greater credence to short term benefits? The Beta-Alpha cycles could take moments to reach resolution, or it could take months, or even years to make a decision. Overly cautious people tend to pay greater attention to long-term benefits. It takes both types for society to function in a healthy manner. But once the decision is made, the supercomputer in our cerebral cortex — right behind our forehead, takes over to form a response.

The purpose of this passage is to explore the Beta-Alpha cycle of critical thinking. But when the brain has burned through its daily dose of *thinking fuel,* it must rest and recuperate. This R&R state is called deep rest, or more commonly, *sleep*. In this state the brain produces Theta waves. Finally, there is an emergency mode, where the brain shuts down all non-essential functions and puts our bodies on life-support. We call this mode, comatose — or coma. The coma state is denoted by Delta waves. Once there, we will stay there until our brain decides it is no longer necessary.

Let's go back to Critical Thinking. Let's say you're in a situation where somebody has communicated something to you that you don't quite understand. Your first decision is going be fight or flight. Do I want to stand and address this, or do I want to leave the vicinity? If you're stuck there, you may be denied the opportunity to do something else that you deem more beneficial. You can tell when a person is in this mode. When you address them, they look at their watch. They are deciding if the information that you are trying to impart is worth their time.

The next mental action is to decide how much time and energy should be invested, if any at all? The next action is to decide what the appropriate response should be. Here's what is looks like.

Mike walks up to John.

"Hey, John, you got a minute?"

John is about to leave for a fishing trip, and thinks, *how long is this gonna take?* He looks at his watch.

"Sure, Mike. What's up?"

If Mike says. "I'm thinking about starting a new business, and I need to run it by you, because I trust your judgement," John is likely to give an entirely different response than if Mike had said, "remember that thousand dollars I owe you?"

That's a clear example. But suppose John didn't understand what Mike said, because he's thinking about largemouth bass. John hears something like, "Blah, blah, blah, new business. Blah, blah, need, something, something . . . thousand dollars. Blah, blah, blah."

Back to not understanding how to respond to a statement. Mr. Abbrect suggests you take a couple seconds to clear the first, and second levels of discernment, and then let your cerebral cortex supercomputer toss out an appropriate response. You do not need to know exactly what to say, and no one will be the wiser, if you just pause to think out your response. The rule is to think out your talk process. Don't talk out your thought process.

I often apply this strategy in my conversations with people. The problem with pausing before you respond is that many people get stuck in the first and second levels of consciousness — stuck in the pause. That extended pause leaves people thinking one of three things; they're being ignored, or that you didn't understand the question, or that you didn't hear them. But first they'll think you didn't understand. Because *they* heard *their self* — and they are much too important to be ignored.

Let's test the theory. Let somebody say something to you that doesn't quite make sense. And don't respond at all to it. Just nod and smile. Eventually they will want to keep talking — trying to convert you to their way of thinking, by convincing you of their intellectual prowess on the topic. You may fully understand what they're talking about. But since you have not expressed your understanding, they will continue to try to make you understand.

Because they think you are stuck in your first or second level of decision making, they have no real interest in questioning you to see if you actually understand. They just to continue to make their point. So, I've let people ramble on, indefinitely, until they stopped and paused and actually asked me if I'm understanding what they're saying. And usually by that time I have heard it, understood what they said, and have *many* well thought out responses. But they won't know that until they stop to actually *care* that I understand.

By this time, in the John and Mike scenario, John knows whether he has time to discuss Mike's business plan, or not. He knows whether Mike is trying to pay him back that thousand dollars, or borrow another thousand, to start his new business. John has allowed himself the opportunity to just pause and listen to what Mike is saying, understand what Mike is saying, and allow his supercomputer to work out the appropriate answer. A knee-jerk response from John's fight or flight cycle could easily damage he and Mike's relationship.

"How bout this Mike," John might answer. "Rather than me loan you another thousand dollars to start your new business, why don't you just keep the thousand you already owe me. Sounds like a great plan."

If you are conversationally stuck in the first or second levels of discernment, and never get to the cerebral cortex, you aren't allowing your brain to fully operate. What I've described to you is a negotiation skill. Let the other person talk. Acknowledge you've heard what they said, with a nod or an, "I see." Then figure out the most appropriate response. And if you talk, repeat what they had to say. Don't talk about your own thoughts and ideas, until after the first and second levels. And then — only after you have an intellectually derived response. Otherwise you'll just end up arguing to protect your ego.

If they perceive you as somebody that did not hear or understand, they will not hear and understand you. So, acknowledge them — summarily, and then let your brain work all the way through the critical thinking process. Give yourself a chance to work out an appropriate response. And then give *them* a chance to get past their first two levels. In this way, you have the conversation you really want to have. When I apply this in my business, I have much better results, and much deeper relationships.

The right brain and left brain both perform beneficial, but different, functions. The three levels of conscious thought are all very different but have important functions. Understanding this, and allowing your brain to work fully, leads to better conclusions and deeper relationships.

Mr. Albrecht urges all of us to engage in critical thinking. Critical thinking leads to critical conversation, which leads to the discovery of viewpoints that you may not have understood before. Or, to solidify facts that you already knew. He encourages each of us to develop this habit. Forgive my terminology, but this way of thinking is the bullshit detector. Install it into your thought process. Is what I'm being told the truth, or an experiential truth, or is it just bullshit? Does the idea or statement represent the truth and actually have merit behind it? If so, how do I determine what that merit is?

Let's look at some of the basic misrepresentations in our society. I'll use an advertising analogy because that's the world I grew up in. We used to have a bunch of commercials about a laundry soap that got rid of "ring around the collar." And if you had a dirty ring inside your shirt collar, it was the result of using an inferior laundry detergent. Therefore, you needed to buy this particular laundry detergent which would eliminate the ring around the inside of your collar.

The critical question is this. Is the ring around the collar a result of laundry detergent or poor hygiene? The answer challenges the commercial with the fact that it's basic hygiene. Wash your neck. Just because the commercial represented their product as the solution, that didn't make it necessarily so. It was total BS.

Just because somebody on TV, radio, Internet or social media presents something as a fact, doesn't make it necessarily so. You have to have that BS detector fully equipped and operational to decide whether you will accept information as a truth, or not. You have to have all three levels of your conscious brain fully engaged, with an understanding that sometimes people's tendencies are more left brained or more right brained. Their experiences can be, and often are, different than yours. Those differences have real value in achieving truth and understanding.

Here are several eye-opening questions. Please answer honestly after each question: always, most of the time, sometimes, never, or explain.

1) Are you more left, or right brain focused? That is to say, are you more creative and abstract. Or are you more logical and analytical?

   _____

2) Once you've decided which one you are, do you equally value the thoughts and ideas from somebody that is opposite brain focused?

   _____

3) Or do you immediately devalue them as somebody that is not worth your time or energy?

   _____

4) Do you objectively listen and acknowledge that people are communicating something that is at least of value to *them?*

   _____

5) When you *do* listen to those people, are you focused on making sure you hear and understand them? Thus, opening the door for *you* to be heard and understood as well?

   _____

6) Do you have your BS detector in place and working?

   _____

7) Are you able to see past emotional statements and objectively pursue the truth?

_____

8) Do you use all the tools and resources available to you to discern the truth?

_____

9) Or do you just stop at what somebody tells you?

_____

10) If your response is generally emotional and without fact, what are you going to do to fix it?

_____

11) Are you open to the idea that sometimes somebody else's truth is *their* truth, even though it may not be yours?

_____

12) Are you comfortable with things being told to you as science, having to pass the scientific method?

_____

If you are willing and able to unite with the collective goal, of us all agreeing on some basic truths, then those truths will set us *all* free. If you can effectively apply this critical thinking into your finances, we can have an honest conversation about how you got where you are, and how to get from there to where you want to be. If you cannot, you will remain where you are.

CHAPTER 13: WHAT REAL WEALTH LOOKS LIKE

In this chapter we want to talk about your goals and dreams. We start this journey with the end in the mind. We want to build your plan based on solid principles so that it can withstand the test of time — those times of plenty, and lack, that we all go through. We'll continue the plan through emotional highs and lows. And we will enjoy the fruits of the plan for the rest of our lives.

Since we are constructing this plan with the end in mind, it makes sense to start by asking this first question. What does financial freedom mean to you? Give it some critical thought and answer below:

_____
_____
_____
_____

Who benefits the most from the successful financial plan you create? Your children? Your community? I don't want to lead you in the answers, but you should in fact know what you're fighting for.

_____
_____
_____
_____
_____

The next question has to do with what motivates you as a human being. Do you just simply want to have a lot of money? _____

If that's the case, you'll find that your motivation will fade and fizzle. Your resolve will not stand through the ups and downs. Pursuing money just for the sake of having money, will only give you happiness for a short period of time. Money should be a tool that is used to build a life. What kind of life do you want to build?

_____
_____
_____
_____
_____

The Bible says that the love of money — not money itself, is the root of all evil. Money, in and of itself, is just a tool — like a tractor or a hammer.

This would be a good time to discuss the meaning of wealth. But first let's ask how *you* define wealth?

_____
_____
_____
_____
_____

The best definition I've heard says that there are five different levels to wealth. From least valuable, to most valuable they are:

1) Monetary wealth — money
2) Proprietary wealth — stuff
3) Relational wealth — mutual love of friends and family
4) Physical wealth — health.
5) Spiritual wealth — God (a higher power)

Money is the *least* of all wealth. If you just have money, and it doesn't do you any good, then it's not really wealth. If you have a bunch of stuff, you'll only be happy until you see better stuff than the stuff you already have. The happiness that comes from possessions is fleeting.

If you have money and possessions, lots of people will love you. You may love them too. But those people that still love you when you're broke are the real treasures. But you won't be able to tell the difference while you have earthly riches. Healthy relationships can last a lifetime. Fare-weather friends flee with the storms in your life.

If you focus on being healthy as a part of your happiness and your overall plan, then those long-term relationships with those treasured people can be long-term. If you have the first four pillars of wealth, adding God will complete your wealth. If all you have is God, you will still have a peaceful life.

I assure you that if you put your focus on God, relationships, and health, and your plan for financial freedom will stand all the trials that come against you. In light of this understanding, answer the question again. What does wealth mean to you?

_____
_____
_____
_____

If your goals are just to make a bunch of money and have lots of stuff eventually, you'll find out that they are not the key to long-term happiness.

When you have a lot of money, what will you do with it? There are no wrong answers, so be honest.

_____
_____
_____
_____
_____

Name the people you will help.

_____	_____
_____	_____
_____	_____
_____	_____
_____	_____

What kind of home will you have?

___

How will you feel in that home?

___

Do you want to live alone or with other people?

___

What does quality time mean for you?

___
___
___

What does quality time mean for you, in relation to the people that you care about?

___
___
___

For me, I'd like to have a family dinner once a week, with everybody freely participating. I want to take a personal vacation *and* a family vacation at least once a year. Those vacations would be in areas that encourage group play and activities. I want to view the people that I care about as blessings in my life and not burdens or responsibilities.

Do you want to travel? If so where to? Why do you want to go there?

___
___
___

For me, I want to see castles in Europe, and lodge there if I can. Champion is an English name, and at one time we had property in England. I would like to find my family homeland. I'd like to share that with somebody. I like the way that castles represent long-term, stable plans and goals that stand the test of centuries.

Do you have a mission, purpose, or calling that has been given to you? Something that adds to the greater good. What is that? Who does it help? Why is that important to you?

_____
_____
_____
_____

Let's examine the book; "7 Habits of Highly Effective People," written by Stephen Covey. One of the principles therein, is to begin with the end in mind. So, I asked myself what do I want people to say about me at my funeral? Think of the funerals you've been to where people have very little to say about someone, other than that they were here. Think about funerals where the people speaking knew, beyond a shadow of a doubt, that the decedents were quality people.

If you were to pass away today, what would the people in your lives have to say about you?

_____
_____
_____
_____

Does the answer to the previous question bring you peace? What do you really want people to say about you at your funeral?

_____
_____
_____
_____

We are doing all this with the goal of setting up a financial plan that supports your mind, body, and spirit. Does what you're doing with your life currently support building a wealthy lifestyle? If so, great. But if not, why not? Is it just because you have poor spending habits? Have you accepted a career that doesn't support your hopes, goals, and dreams? Are you currently working to build somebody else's hopes and dreams at the expense of your own? If that is the case, we will discuss other options later in this book. Right now, we are just setting goals.

In your best estimation, how much money will it take to achieve the lifestyle we talked about in this chapter so far? _____

Do you want to just take care of your lifetime, or do you want to pass on intergenerational wealth that keeps going forever? _____

The best definition of insanity is continuing to do the same things, over and over again, and expecting different results. To build your own dreams you may have to change some things. Habits that you may not even be aware of may be at the root of your financial woes. And here's a good rule about change. Pain does not come from change. Pain comes from *resisting* change. The tough times of life will come and go. The good times will come and go. Change is inevitable. Whatever our circumstance — this too shall pass. If we let it.

Just look at the trillion-dollar anti-aging industry. Make-up, plastic surgery, hair care, mid-life crisis spending, and the like drain the resources of the very people that need to be saving as much money as the can. Some go so far that they become a grotesque caricature of their younger self. Some even die in the pursuit of everlasting youth.

If something made you feel good at one time, but it's making you miserable now, wouldn't it just be better to let it go? Look at the trillion-dollar pleasure industries — the feel-good merchants. The peddlers of alcohol, drugs, tabaco, sex, and other thrill products continue taking money from people too numb to even get high. Their pleasure ends in addiction — the ultimate insanity. Many die in the pursuit of that first high.

What will your legacy be? Will future generations care about the causes you supported? Or will you die in the pursuit of vain-glory, or pleasure, squandering what might have created a legacy of wealth for generations to come?

In the space below I want you to make a mission statement, using your best answers from the questions above, to serve as a launch pad for your financial plan. Write your mission statement in a single paragraph. Once that is done, we can start building the actual financial plan.

_____
_____
_____
_____
_____

Answer the following questions as honestly and as accurately as you can. Dishonest answers will only drive your plan astray. There is no judgment here. There is no obligation to impress anyone with your answers.

Table 4: Family Balance Sheet

1	Your last year's salary before taxes	_____
2	Spouse's last year's salary before taxes	_____
3	Other live-ins' last year's salaries before taxes	_____
4	Your yearly IRA or 401(k) contributions	_____
5	Spouse's yearly IRA or 401(k) contributions	_____
6	Other live-ins' yearly IRA or 4101(k) contributions	_____
7	Your yearly health insurance bill	_____
8	Spouse's yearly health insurance bill	_____
9	Other live-ins' yearly health insurance bills	_____
10	What you actually paid in taxes last year	_____
11	What your spouse actually paid in taxes last year	_____
12	What other live-ins' actually paid in taxes last year	_____
13	Yearly household mortgage (only) payment	_____
14	Yearly homeowner's insurance bill	_____
15	Yearly home property tax bill	_____
16	Household expenditures on miscellaneous medical costs	_____
17	Annual household grocery bill	_____
18	Annual household restaurant bill	_____
19	Your annual car note	_____
20	Spouse's annual car note	_____
21	Other live-ins' annual car note	_____
22	Your annual car insurance bill	_____
23	Spouse's annual car insurance bill	_____
24	Other live-ins' annual car insurance bills	_____

25	Household annual gasoline expenditure	_____
26	Your yearly salary before taxes	_____
27	Spouse's year salary before taxes	_____
28	Other live-ins' yearly salaries before taxes	_____
29	Household annual internet bill	_____
30	Annual landline telephone bill	_____
31	Household annual cell phone bill	_____
32	Annual electric bill	_____
33	Annual water bill	_____
33	Annual gas bill	_____
35	Annual trash collection bill	_____
36	Annual landscaping bill	_____
37	Annual swimming pool maintenance bill	_____
38	Your last year's life insurance bill	_____
39	Spouse's last year's life insurance bill	_____
40	Other live-ins' last year's life insurance bills	_____
41	Your last's year's credit card payments	_____
42	Spouse's last year's credit card payments	_____
43	Other live-ins' last year's credit card payments	_____
44	Last year's household vacation cost	_____
45	Last year's household outside entertainment costs	_____
46	Household recreational drug use cost	_____
47	Your last year's savings	_____
48	Spouse's last year's savings	_____
49	Other live-ins' last year's savings	_____

To get the total picture of your household cashflow, calculate the following:

+ Add lines one, two, and three for total household income: _____
+ Add lines 4 through 46 for household expenses: _____
- Subtract expenses from income: _____
+/- Is your cashflow positive or negative: _____
+ Add lines 47, 48, and 49 for total household savings: _____

And there you have it — your financial life in a nutshell. Are you happy with your nut? Divide by 12, to get the monthly cashflow.

Some of you may be scratching your head right now. Your analysis shows that you have a surplus, every month, but your bank account is still zero. What happened to the rest of it? Well that is the question; isn't it? Money — like water will find its way to the floor. If you're not paying attention it will eventually *corrode* holes in the floor and *erode* the foundation. The *corrosion* is caused by bad spending habits. The resulting *erosion* is your dwindling, or nonexistent savings account.

How does your monthly surplus, if you have one, get spent rather than added to your savings? Let's look for the lost loot, that could easily go to savings. What do you spend on entertainment, monthly? Do you frequent expensive coffee shops? Do you shop for clothes with money you should be saving? Do you pay membership fees? What other unnecessary indulgences do you allow yourself? Do you tithe? If you eliminate the unnecessary spending, you might be able to tithe *and save,* as well.

Do you pay yourself first? Let me explain what that means. Most people do in fact have a savings and checking account. Most people put everything they earn into their checking account. Then they pay all those people waiting in line for their money. The mortgage, or rent, the bills etc. Then if there's anything left over, they might transfer it to their savings account. How much is always left over at the end of the month? Zero; right? Most people pay everybody else first. And if anything is left, they *might* pay themselves. But usually they waste the excess on something of little or no value.

In the spirit of paying yourself first, we need for you to incorporate your goals, both collectively and individually. This would be for you and your spouse to decide. Think of one six-month goal. Then a one-year goal. After that, come up with a five-year personal goal for yourself, and another one for your spouse? Write the answers on the following page.

Table 5: Family Goals

Six Month Goal
_____
_____

One Year Goal
_____
_____

Your Five-Year Personal Goal
_____
_____
_____

Spouse's Five-Year Personal Goal
_____
_____
_____

Circle all those goals with red ink. What is one long-range goal that you and your spouse want for yourselves and for the family? Write the answer below and circle it.

Long Range Family Goal
_____
_____
_____
_____
_____
_____

Now I want you to draw an outline around all of those goals, and title that a whole box your dream account. That is what your savings account is. It is you and your family's dreams. In the *pay yourself first* model, all the family's income should be deposited into your dreams account first.

From the 49-question cash flow analysis, you should decide how much you need to spend every month on your bills. This should include groceries and miscellaneous purchase's as well.

Now that all of the money is going to feeding your dreams first, you have indeed paid yourself first. Then, on the first of the month, transfer the estimated amount that you need for your bills into the bill account. Then pay all the other people waiting in line from that.

Let me give an example from my home. Our family bills are about $3500 a month. We make a good deal more than that as a family. All of our money goes into our dream account. And then, on the first of each month, we transfer the $3500 into the bill account. Our monthly goal is to not spend the whole $3500. The less we spend the less we have to transfer from our dreams the next month, and the more that gets to stay in our dreams. So, if we only spend $3300 of the $3500, then we only have to transfer $3300 to the bill account the next month.

We pay ourselves first and everybody else second, because we have made our goals and dreams the priority for our money. The plan helps us cut out wasteful spending and eliminate impulse shopping. Let's say there's nothing wrong with my wardrobe right now. And I'm walking past a sale at the mall. If I've already spent all the money in the bill account for the month, and I really want that new shirt, I can actually have that shirt without having to put it on a credit card. I would first have to transfer money from the dream account to the bill account, in order to be able to spend it. Just having to do that extra step is usually enough to steer me away from an impulse buy.

Moreover, I can generally have anything I want, anytime I want it. But if we've already used up all the money in the bill account, I have to steal from my family goals and dreams account to satisfy my wants. Do you pay yourself first?

CHAPTER 14: BREAKING THE DEPT TRAP

Figure 19: Quit Playing the Rigged Game

If you really want to be debt free and have your money work for you instead of the bankers, you must be disciplined about how you spend your money. Discipline simply means training your body and mind. So, when it becomes evident that you are financial unhealthy, you have to develop certain disciplines to become financially healthy. So, let's develop your financially healthy discipline program now.

Now that your goals and dreams are listed, bills itemized, and you've identified places where your money gets away, it's time to plan. Your plan begins with an honest monthly budget, and a true assessment of your actual income. Your total income goes into your dream savings account. Transfer your budget into the bill paying account on the first of each month. Discipline yourself not to spend money in a way that does not match what goals. Let's tackle your debt now.

These are some of the services we provide:

- Improve your credit score 120-200 points in six months
- Reduce the interest on current debt
- Credit Report Analysis

We will help you reduce credit card debt, personal Loan debt, business debts, medical bills, and private student loans by negotiating as follows:

- What are you actually on the hook for?
- Settle for a fraction of what you owe!
- Average savings of $17,200.
- Good credit when done!
- Stop paying ridiculous amounts of interest.
- Stop paying a balance that never goes down.
- Eliminate debt on items you no longer have access to.
- Reduce your Debt to Income Ratio.
- You've probably paid for what you bought, two times over.

You must first come to grips with your current situation. Run your debts through the debt calculator link. Total up how much you will pay in principal and interest if you keep doing what you're doing now. Add in how much you have already paid on this debt and then ask yourself this question. If you had known then what you just learned, would you have still done it?

Know this about banks and credit cards. YOU ARE NOT THEIR CUSTOMERS. The board of directors and shareholders are. You are the means through which they serve their customers. Their job is to keep you in debt and milk you for as much interest as they can.

STOP THE INSANITY! FIGHT BACK! Find out how much we can put back into your pocket. Anybody attempting to entice you into paying with credit, is doing it for profit, because they care about their lender. The banks customers are the Board of Directors and shareholders — *not you*. Quit playing their game. The deck is stacked like a game in Vegas — it's always rigged so the house wins. They are *always* trying to take away from your goals and dreams, to meet their profit margin.

So, what do you do, now that your debt situation seems hopeless? You fight back, that's what you do. And you don't do it alone. You'll never get out of a problem by using the thought process that created it in first place. You must improve your cash flow by doing everything legally possible to cut your payments towards debt and prioritize that money back into your savings plan. And you must change your mind-set about credit. Lending agencies are not your friend. They are financial predators.

Debt Consolidation

There are several programs that help consolidate you away from high interest rates — essentially just creating one debt for another. Even if the payments are lower, it doesn't consider all of the money you paid towards interest on the initial loan. Use the debt calculator on the website provided earlier — you'll see that even the new debtors can make a lot of money off your consolidation.

And while your monthly payments on the debt may be reduced, they get to collect interest for a longer period of time. Consolidation is good sometimes — if you have a quick plan to pay off the debt before you pay too much interest. If you're considering a consolidation loan, first calculate everything you've paid towards that debt already — principal and interest. Then calculate how much you would pay on the remaining principal, with interest, in the consolidation program to see if it's actually worth considering.

Refinancing your house can be another option. But remember what we talked about before. Let's say the original mortgage was $300,000. And, that you've been paying on it for 10 years. You've already paid $120,000 in interest on that mortgage because it's frontloaded — amortized. If you refinance and take a $40,000 equity loan. you have a new $340,000 mortgage that's gonna cost you another $170,000 in interest, because you've re-amortized. All that adds up to about $290,000 in interest, on a $340,000 loan. Does that seem wise? I think not.

Take the following Six Steps to Financial Freedom:

1: Federal Student Loan Forgiveness Program Applications

- Do you owe more than $10,000?
- Special programs for public service employees.
- Check program qualification.
- Save thousands.

2: Private Student Loan Negotiating

- What are you actually on the hook for?
- Settle for a fraction of what you owe!
- Average savings of $23,900.
- Good credit when done!

3: Budget Counseling

Do you have more month than money? Money is like water. It will find its way down and out if you don't fix the leaks. If there is too little water, everyone around you withers or leaves you. If there is too much — without a plan, it will erode and ruin everything you've built. Get a grip on your cash flow. Find the leaks and stop them. Direct it where you want it to go and make it grow!

4: Life Insurance, Annuities, Final Expense

- Protect your Assets.
- Replace your income.
- Tax Advantaged Retirement.
- Save for college.
- Protect savings from market losses.

5: Financial Plans and Dream Maps

Do you want to…
- Travel?
- Volunteer?
- Retire Young?
- Own your home outright?
- Start a business or non-profit?

6: Start Your Own Business

Starting a business is great way to increase cash flow and get a tax write off. You cannot prioritize the banks profit over your family's well-being. You *should not* care about protecting your credit score, by using credit to pay two or three times the cost of the products you buy. You will never get out of debt by going deeper in debt.

Student Loans

There are two types of student loans; federally backed student loans and private student loans. Yes, the idea of getting an education is a good one. But if you take one of these loans and never earn enough money to pay it off, you'll join about 22 million people that are in the same boat. Let's start with the federal student loans.

How Federal Student Loans Work

One of the benefits of federal student loans is the fact you don't need a credit check, in most cases. Only PLUS loans require a credit check. Otherwise, anyone who attends school can receive federal student loans. No need to prove income, credit standing, or even get your parents to cosign. Once you receive your financial aid letter, you need to decide if you will accept the package. Understanding how federal student loans work can help you decide whether they are right for you.

Understand that you will pay interest on student loan debt. With federal loans, the interest rate is set by Congress each year. Each academic year, you get a new loan, with an interest rate that remains fixed for the term of the loan. By the end of your time in school, you will have several student loans with different interest rates.

With a subsidized student loan, the federal government pays the interest on your loan while you are enrolled in school (at least half-time), as well as during the grace period after graduation. For all other federal loans, the government does not pay your interest while you are in school. Instead, interest accrues the whole time you are at college. At the end, the accrued interest gets added to the principal balance at the end of your grace period. When that happens, you end up paying interest on interest. The good news is you can prevent this from happening by making payments on the interest before the grace period ends.

How Private Student Loans Work

Private student loans require an application directly to the bank, credit union, or other lender. Qualifying will depend on your credit history and could require a cosigner. When you receive your financial aid award letter, it may also include a list of *private* student loan lenders. Even if you don't receive information about private student loans in the award letter, it's important to be aware of the option.

Interest rates for private student loans can be fixed or variable. The interest *type* (fixed or variable) and interest *rate* depends on the lender, your credit rating, and other qualifying factors. Realize that interest not only accrues while you are in school, but you might also be required to make payments before you graduate (something that's never required of you for federal student loans). Check with your lender to see if you can defer your student loan repayment until after you graduate. Some private lenders even offer a grace period.

These loans don't just go away because you can't pay them. Federally backed student loans are issued and held by a bank that is privately owned and operated and backed by the federal government. Thus, the IRS has power to collect.

Fortunately, the federal government has created programs that protect you from the predatory lending practices of those banks. They are called income-based repayment programs. These programs were created by the William D. Ford Act in 1997. They have essentially made a large pool of money, available for people that have federally backed student loans, during times of hardship.

The federal government will give you a new monthly payment, based strictly on your income and household size. They will also give you a new term, if you made the payments for the term originally given to you. The new term could be between 120 and 300 months. And the remaining balance and interest can be eliminated.

These programs are great because your payment is based on a percentage of income, with deductions for minor children or people sharing the cost of the residence. I've seen payments as low as zero dollars a month, because of extraordinary hardships. But it will always be based on a percentage of your income, so it will never be an excessive payment. If you apply for the program and are approved, there is one condition. Every year, you must recertify based on your current income and household size. But the sooner you start the clock, the better off you'll be.

Special student forgiveness programs are also in place for public service employees. This includes anybody that works for a government or nonprofit entity. These programs currently have a repayment term of 10 years. The existing program's terms and conditions will be modified, by the new administration, starting in 2020.

Anybody working for a private for-profit entity is likely to currently have a 200 to 300 a month repayment term. Having that term does not mean you don't have an opportunity to pay off the loan sooner than that if you want to. It just means that you have a protected payment for that timeframe, and forgiveness at the end of the timeframe if you need it. Therefore, you are protected from the predatory lending practices of banks.

Case Study

I recently processed a case for a young couple that had $45,000 in federally back student loans. The husband is the pastor of a church, so he qualifies for the Public Service Loan Forgiveness Program for 120 months. His original loans totaled $21,000. Their combined income is $27,000 a year. They have three small children, and the wife just started her marriage and family counseling practice. The husband was paying $220 a month for his student loans. And she was paying $200 on hers.

This was causing extreme hardship in their house. We qualified him for a zero-dollar monthly payment for the next 12 months. We also started the 120-month clock towards loan forgiveness. We were also able to give her a zero dollar a month payment for the next 12 months.

The hope is that her practice will continue to grow along with his church. And that their income continues to grow as well. So, let's say next year their income goes up to $55,000, and they still have three children. Their combined student loan payments would be somewhere around $140 a month for the next 12 months. Let's say the year after that, they still made about $55,000 combined, but they had another child. There payment would drop to about $115 a month.

For making those payments, three years are taken off the loan forgiveness term clock. The point is that they will always have a protected payment and a light at the end of the tunnel, for the loans to go away.

With the extra $420 a month we were able to save them, they established their emergency fund/dream account. They have a fresh start and the ability to live a debt free life. This is just one example of how Loan Forgiveness Programs can work in your favor.

Loan Forgiveness Programs

How much in student loan forgiveness can you receive? This depends on the loan forgiveness program you apply to. In some cases, you may even qualify for up to 100% loan forgiveness. Below, you'll find a list of all federal student loan forgiveness programs, as well as some state options.

Public Service Loan Forgiveness

The Public Service Loan Forgiveness Program (PSLF) offers complete loan forgiveness to those who work in the public sector. This includes non-profit employees, Peace Corps volunteers, public school teachers and staff, and government employees, to name a few.

How Much in Loan Forgiveness can I Receive from PSLF?

You may qualify for complete student loan forgiveness after 10 years. Or, 120 payments instead of the standard 20 to 25-year forgiveness term. There is no dollar cap on the amount of money that you can have forgiven through PSFL. Any qualifying loan balance that remains after 10 years is forgiven in its entirety. Best of all, the IRS does not view the forgiven debt as taxable income.

Who is Eligible for PSLF?

The PSLF program cares more about who you work for rather than what you do. To qualify, you must work or volunteer for one of the following:

- A government organization at any level.
- A tax-exempt 501(c)(3) not-for-profit organization.
- A not-for-profit organization that provides qualifying public services.
- Program participants must also work full-time.

You are considered a full-time worker if your employer considers you a fulltime employee. Or, if you work a minimum of 30 hours per week, whichever is greater. You must also be paying in an income-driven repayment plan to qualify.

The Public Service Loan Forgiveness program forgives any non-defaulted loan borrowed under the William D. Ford Federal Direct Loan Program. Other loans like Federal Perkins Loans or Federal Family Education Loans can become eligible for PSLF if you consolidate them into a Direct Consolidated Loan. You will not officially apply for PSLF until after you make 120 qualifying payments while working in an eligible job. Completing and submitting the Employment Certification form is the only way to ensure you are making qualifying payments. You should submit this form annually, and again every time you switch jobs.

You must also ensure that your loans are in the Direct Loan Program. Payments made to an IBR, ICR, PAYE, or REPAYE, count as qualifying payments for those who work in the public sector and would like to apply for public service loan forgiveness

The Teacher Loan Forgiveness Program (TLFP)

TLFP is a form of student loan forgiveness that is separate from the Direct Student Loan or Obama Student Loan Forgiveness Program. This program awards educators with a principal reduction of their federal loans. It was designed to encourage students to enter the education field and to incentivize teachers to continue teaching.

How Much in Loan Forgiveness can I Receive from TLFP?

TLFP is one of the best student loan forgiveness options. Qualifying teachers receive a tax-exempt principal reduction of either $5,000, or $17,500, on their federal loans. This drops their overall loan balance, making monthly loan payments smaller and thus more manageable. For some teachers, this eliminates their federal student loan balance altogether.

The TLFP allows teachers to remain eligible for the Public Service Loan Forgiveness Program. Under this program, their remaining federal loan balance would be forgiven after 10 years of on-time payments. This means teachers get a principal reduction after five years, and then complete forgiveness after an additional 10 years. Compared to the standard forgiveness term of 20 to 25 years, this is a great option.

Who is Eligible for TLFP?

Qualified applicants must have worked as a teacher for five consecutive years. One of these years must be after the 1997-98 academic year. This program defines a teacher as anyone who teaches directly in a classroom or does classroom-type teaching outside of the classroom. These teachers must work at an elementary school, secondary school, or educational service agency that serves low-income students. Special education teachers qualify too. Teachers must also meet eligibility criteria that deem them highly qualified. Highly qualified teachers must have:

- At least a bachelor's degree.
- Received full state certification as a teacher.
- Not had licensure or certification requirements waived for any reason.

Along with meeting the above criteria, teachers must prove their subject knowledge and teaching skills. Elementary school teachers must pass a rigorous state test on basic elementary school curriculum like writing, math, and reading. Middle and secondary teachers must pass a state academic subject test, earn a certification, or degree in the subjects they teach.

Not only does the teacher have to qualify, but their federal loans must qualify too. The loans must have been taken out before you finish your five years of consecutive teaching service. You can only seek forgiveness for the following loan types:

- Direct Subsidized Loans
- Direct Unsubsidized Loans
- Subsidized Federal Stafford Loans
- Unsubsidized Federal Stafford Loans

Find out if you're eligible for Teacher Loan Forgiveness. Unlike other student loan forgiveness programs, you apply for the Teacher Loan Forgiveness program *after* completing your five consecutive years of service and not before. So, if you have already worked five qualifying years, you can apply and receive teacher loan forgiveness today. If you worked at more than one school during your five years of consecutive service, you must fill out an application for each school.

Total and Permanent Disability Discharge Program (TPD)

TPD helps borrowers suffering from a disability by offering a complete discharge on their federal loans. Unfortunately, most private lenders do not offer disability discharge. The few that do are Sallie Mae, Wells Fargo, Discover, and New York Higher Education Services Corp.

How much in Loan Forgiveness can I Receive from TPD?

If accepted for the disability discharge, you would receive complete loan forgiveness. You will no longer owe any money in either principal or interest. Best of all, the amount forgiven is not reported as income to the IRS as of 2018. This means you will not have to pay taxes on it and will not lose your eligibility for government programs like social security or Medicare. Along with immediate discharge, you might also receive some of your money back. Lenders are required to return any money that you paid on your loan since the start of your disability.

Who is eligible for TPD?

To receive immediate disability discharge, qualifying borrowers must prove that they are totally and permanently disabled. You must have documentation from the Veterans Affairs Office, the Social Security Office, or your physician. The burden of proof is high and relies heavily on that official documentation. In general, you have to have been disabled for at least 60 months or expect to be disabled for at least 60 months to qualify.

Those with disabilities expected to result in death are also eligible. Your loans must be eligible too. TPD discharge relieves you from repaying loans made under the:

- William D. Ford Federal Direct Loan Program
- Federal Family Education Loan Program
- Federal Perkins Loan Program

TPD discharge also relieves borrowers from their TEACH Grant service obligation. You can start the application process online by visiting the Federal Student Aid website. You can also apply by filling out a form and have your doctor certify your disability.

Bankruptcy and Undue Hardship Student Loan Discharge

It is rare, but it is possible to have your student loans discharged through bankruptcy. This process requires proving "undue hardship" and may even require hiring a student loan lawyer. What are the benefits of bankruptcy discharge? If you can prove "undue hardship", the court has several options. In most cases, the proceedings will result in one of the following:

- Your loans are fully discharged, and you no longer have to make any payments.
- Your loans are partially discharged, and you must repay a portion of the loan.
- Your loan takes on new terms, like a lower interest rate or a longer repayment term. You must still repay your loan.

Who is Eligible for Bankruptcy and Undue Hardship Discharge?

To discharge your student loans through bankruptcy, you must prove that paying back your loans would be an undue hardship. Unfortunately, there is no universal definition for "undue hardship." Many courts will use the Brunner Test to determine whether you meet the burden of proof for undue hardship. To pass this test, you need to meet the following three criteria:

- Based on your current financial situation, paying back your loan would make it impossible for you to maintain a minimal standard of living for yourself and your family.
- Your current financial situation is persistent and will continue for a large part of your loan repayment period.
- You have made a good faith effort and done what you can to repay your student loans. Some courts will look at your income, expenses, loan amount, and other circumstances to make a determination.

The best way to find out how courts in your jurisdiction define "undue hardship" is to speak with a local bankruptcy attorney.

How to get my Loans Discharged through Bankruptcy?

If you have decided that bankruptcy is the best option, you will first need to choose between Chapter 7 and Chapter 13 bankruptcy. Chapter 7 is for borrowers who have no income to spare for paying back debt, and the Chapter 13 is for borrowers who have some money to pay back some of their debt. Since bankruptcy does not typically include student loan debt, you will then need to file a bankruptcy adversary proceeding. This proceeding asks the court to determine whether student loan repayment would cause undue hardship. Be aware that these proceedings take a while and can get expensive. You can always consider applying for federal repayment plans or student loan forgiveness programs instead.

Student Loan Interest Student Loan Forgiveness

In the Direct Loan Program, interest in the IBR [Discussed in 'Who is Eligible for Public Service Loan Forgiveness?'] does not capitalize on the subsidized portion of your direct loan. This applies only for the first three years of your IBR payment, and only if your IBR payment is less than what is normally due to interest. This can amount to many thousands of dollars depending on your loan balance and what type of payment you currently qualify for. There is also interest forgiveness in the PAYE and REPAYE plans as well.

Student Loan Interest Deduction and Forgiveness Student Loan Forgiveness

If you enroll into any of the income-driven repayment plans, at the end of the loan term, your remaining loan balance would be forgiven. The term of the loan would be between 20 to 25-years, depending on which repayment plan you choose, and when your loans were originally borrowed. How much you will be forgiven will depend on your original loan amount, how much you are earning, and how much your earnings fluctuate during your repayment term.

Parent PLUS Loan Discharge

Parent Plus Loans are eligible for discharge if either the student or parent passes away. To begin the discharge process, a family member or legal representative must supply a copy of the death certificate to either the college or the loan servicer.

Closed School Discharge

Colleges and universities do not commonly close, but it does happen. Luckily, in those situations, borrowers are protected thanks to the closed school discharge. What are the benefits? This program relieves students of their federal student debt if they are unable to attain their degree because their college or university closed down. You will no longer have to make payments on eligible federal student loans and any payments you already made will be refunded. If you were in default on any of these loans, the loan holder will also repair your damaged credit history.

Private Student Loan Negotiation

Private Student Loans are not backed by the federal government. They are an unsecured debt like personal loans or credit cards. With all unsecured loans or credit cards you have the right and the ability to negotiate these debts.

The majority of my business involves helping people seeking counseling for credit card debt or private student loans. And I will always be in favor of hiring somebody that negotiates professionally — should they be over $10,000. Those under $10,000, you can often negotiate them yourself. To do this you're going to have to sacrifice your credit score and your peace of mind for six months to a year.

They won't negotiate with somebody that's being a good little sheep — those that care about their credit score, and don't mind paying relentless interest, forever. You have to use every legal means to get them to the table to negotiate. And that's going to involve you standing your ground and letting them know that you will no longer play their game.

We are not saying that you shouldn't payback a reasonable amount for your debt. But you shouldn't pay back double, or triple what you borrowed, because that is unjust. We generally settle people's debt for 60 cents on the dollars that they currently owe, in a 2 to 6-year term. Thus, paying back 60% of what you owe now, rather than 250% of the original debt.

If you do not have an emergency fund to leverage, we can set up programs that can catch up payments all the way down to about a third of what you're paying now. Thus, allowing you to add to your savings with the extra amount.

A couple I just helped has two small children. The husband is in sales and his wife is a teacher. They found themselves with about $39,000 in credit card debt, while trying to keep up with the cost of the house and the kids. They had been paying about $1200 a month on their debt for the last two and half years, and the balance isn't going down. Early last year the husband had some medical issues and wasn't able to work, which caused an increase in debt.

We put them into a program that settled the $39,000 debt for $21,000 over the next six years, at a payment of $395 a month rather than $1,200. They promised themselves that they would save the extra $800 a month. If so, they will have saved $10,000 by the end of the year. At that point they can cover the cost of any emergencies that come without having to use the credit cards ever again. Another family saved.

There are drawbacks to the debt negotiation programs. You will immediately cease paying directly to the lenders and the money you pay will be put into a third-party account, or escrow account, for the negotiator to use. It can take up to six months, or more, for the banks to be willing to negotiate. During that six months your credit will tank, and they will do everything in their power to try to scare you into making the payments the way they want you to.

A professional negotiator will know how to navigate the process and get the banks to come to the table. Eventually your creditors will realize that it's better to take something rather than nothing. The professional negotiator also knows the loopholes and illegalities in the banks' contracts and has ways to use those illegalities as leverage.

SECTION TWO: FINANCIAL PRODUCTS

DISCLAIMER: The information provided in SECTION TWO of "THE DEBT TRAP" is intended to provide general information only. And the information has been prepared without taking into account any particular person's objectives, financial situation or needs. Before acting on such information, you should consider the appropriateness of the information, your personal objectives, financial situation or needs. In particular, you should obtain professional advice before acting on the information contained in this section.

No representation or warranty is made as to the accuracy, completeness or reliability of any estimates, opinions, conclusions or other information contained on this section. This section may contain certain positive statements. Positive statements are not guarantees of future performance. The products to be discussed involve known and unknown risks, uncertainties and other factors You should not place reliance on positive statements.

To the maximum extent permitted by law, we disclaim all liability and responsibility for any direct or indirect loss or damage which may be suffered as a result of relying on anything in this section, including any positive statements. Past performance is not an indication of future performance.

CHAPTER 15: LIFE INSURANCE

Let's get to the nuts and bolts of financial security. If you've read this far, then that's why you're here. But why are you here — in the sense of on this earth? I believe we are put here to contribute to the good of those in our sphere of influence — starting with our family. To most of us, our immediate family is our top priority. And why do we all have an innate desire to produce, protect, and prosper our biological children? Ahhhh — that's the question. You feel it in your very bones.

We were built that way. It's in our DNA. Eat, work, reproduce, protect. That DNA in us wants to live forever. And so do we. Our children carry our DNA — and us, into the future. There is an unbroken chain of reproduction, from every living person on the planet, back to the first of our species. Through our children, we live forever. You may not have ever thought about it that way. But the more they look like you, the more you love them. And don't we feel the greatest thrill when someone says, "he (or she) looks just like you."

Point established. Let's move on to the nuts and bolts of financial security.

LIFE INSURANCE

A life insurance policy has four constituents.

1) Insurance Company
2) Policy Owner
3) Person Insured
4) Beneficiary

The life insurance policy itself is a contract between the policy owner and the insurance company. The policy owner pays insurance premiums to the insurance company, to compensate the beneficiary, if the person insured dies while the policy is in effect. The owner of the policy may, or may not, be the person whose life is insured. The owner of the policy may, or may not, be the beneficiary.

Life insurance policies can be complicated and may have many optional components called riders. Make sure you talk to a properly licensed insurance professional to help you understand your options BEFORE you purchase a life insurance policy.

LIFE INSURANCE UNDERWRITING

Nearly all types of life insurance require the person whose life is being insured to undergo a sort of background check by an 'underwriter', prior to the issuance of a policy. Insurance companies are risk averse. They are in business to make money. They would prefer to insure people that are young, healthy, and financially stable. And thus, the underwriting process.

First and foremost, they want to determine the quality of your health. A paramedic tech will come to your home to measure your blood pressure, see — in person how much you weight, draw blood, urine, and give you a stool sample kit. They will ask you a list of health questions — some of which you may not want to answer. But you have to.

If they ask if you smoke, and you say no, nicotine will show up in your sample. And you will be 'rated' (increased premium) accordingly. If you are overweight, you will be rated. If one of your parents died of cancer, you will be rated. If there are too many adverse medical issues, the underwriter will decline your policy.

Your policy may be rated, or declined, based on your lifestyle. If you have drunk driving arrests, you will be rated. If you just got out of prison, the price of insurance goes up through the rating process. A tobacco user will pay two and a half times the premium of a non-smoker.

All of this information will be uploaded to an insurance information exchange, for other insurance companies to see — for the rest of your life. You won't be able to come back and change your story. If you are declined by one insurance company, the other insurance companies will know.

The underwriting process can be challenging to the point of being emotionally brutal. So, when you are granted a policy, you may want to think long and hard before you cancel it. I have seen people cancel a life insurance policy and become uninsurable soon after.

TERM LIFE INSURANCE

Life insurance makes a poor man wealthy. Even if you are still in debt, there is no reason not to have it. A lot of good people look at life insurance as a burial policy, and not much more. And those that see it that way place a very low priority on having it. Their rationale goes something like this:

"Cremation is cheap these days. Surely my family and friends can scrape together a few thousand dollars."

If that thought even crosses your mind, your family can't — and you have the wrong friends.

Life insurance is worth more than a burial. An affordable life insurance policy can replace your future income for the next 30 years. Believe it or not, I've heard the following statement:

"But what do I get at the end of the 30 years?"

That's not the point. And the people that think like that don't even want to get *the* point.

The point is this. If you are a middle-class parent with young children, and you die before they are grown, those children will grow up in poverty. It is a certainty. If you are already struggling to put food on the table, and you die prematurely, your children will live in squalor — period. And that is as easily avoidable, as the certainty of death. Knowing that, your family will hate you for not protecting them beyond your own mortality.

Say you and your spouse have two children in middle school. Being a modern adult, in the 21st century, your family has four cellphones. Being a cautious consumer, you have replacement insurance for all four phones. Let's say it's a no-brainer at 60 bucks a month. But I hear those same good folks say they can't afford life insurance. That, in my opinion is absurd to the point of idiocy. Here's why. If you are reasonably healthy, here's what a 60 dollar a month life insurance policy can do for your family.

1) Pay off your debt.
2) Pay down your mortgage.
3) Send both kids *through* college.
4) Give your spouse the ability to maintain the family's current lifestyle.
5) Bury your cheap ass.

6) Bury your child, should you survive them.

Having said all that, and even insulted some of you, purchasing life insurance can be a daunting task. But it doesn't have to be. Even If your children are toddlers — or even if you don't yet have children — but want to. A simple 30-year term policy, with child riders (child burial insurance) will cover all six of the above needs. It works because life insurance favors the young and healthy. If you survived your upbringing and have a living wage job, you are young and healthy.

Hold on. I'm going to run a quote for a healthy 25-year-old male. A top-ten insurance company quotes a simple 25-year term life at $50.31 for a half-million dollars of coverage. What could a 25-year-old married male forego to come up with $50 dollars per month?

1) One movie date.
2) Ten beers at the fancy pub.
3) Yoga lessons.
4) A weekend of golf.
5) A night out with the boys.
6) One cheap restaurant bill.

No need to belabor the point. But if you are ten years into your career, and 35-years old, you can afford a higher premium. And *that*, my friends, is the power of term-life insurance. And that should be the foundation of the financial *house*, metaphorically speaking, that will sustain your family's future.

CASH VALUE WHOLE LIFE INSURANCE

On to other policies for other needs. Your need to have your life insured does not go away just because your term life policy has expired. Older people are statistically more likely to die than younger people. Therefore, the cost of life insurance is far more expensive when you are older. The coverage purchased by the 25-year-old, for $50 per month, will cost $390 per month at 55-years-old.

Whole life insurance policies lower the older age premiums by increasing the younger age premiums. Thus, averaging out the cost of the monthly payments. You'll pay more while you're young, in order to pay less when you're older. The younger and healthier you are when you purchase whole life, the lower the monthly premiums will be. Remember that life insurance policies favor the young and healthy and penalize the old and sick. The insurance companies are able to charge less when you're young because they'll be collecting premium payments longer.

UNIVERSAL LIFE INSURANCE

In times past, a whole life policy meant fixed premium — fixed death benefit — fixed interest rate. Instead of going through the history of whole life insurance, let's discuss the current state of the industry. Many, if not most, insurance companies and their policy owners prefer a modified whole life instrument called Universal Life. The reason being, its flexibility. While the traditional Whole Life contract had fixed premium, death benefit, and interest rate, the Universal contract allows the policy owner to vary all three parameters. Why would a policy owner want to do that?

1) In times of plenty, the policy owner can increase his or her premium payment (to a point) to build cash value faster.
2) In times of lack, the policy owner can decrease his premium payment (to a point) or even miss payments (under certain circumstances).
3) Increased cash value increases the death benefit, allowing the policy owner to start out with a less than desirable face value.
4) The policy owner can select the cash value investment type that suits his or her risk tolerance (greater risk — greater potential reward).

Another benefit of the Universal policy is the tax-free loan feature. The policy owner may borrow money, using the accumulated cash value as collateral. They can choose to pay back the loan at their discretion — or never pay it back at all. When the insured person dies, the loan is subtracted from the death benefit payout.

Therefore, the policy owner may use a Universal Life policy as a tax-free retirement or savings account. The longer the cash account goes untouched, the bigger the nest egg will be at retirement. One could even set up monthly tax-free distributions. That's equivalent to a self-directed, tax free pension.

INDEXED UNIVERSAL LIFE INSURANCE

Here's where cash value investment *type* comes into play. The accumulated cash value can be tied to a stock market exchange index, like the American DOW, S&P, or Nasdaq indices — or a Global ensemble combining indices such as the Hang-Seng, NEKKEI, DAX, and Emerging (risky) markets. A risk averse policy owner may eliminate market risk altogether by choosing a fixed interest rate.

By tuning these variables (premium, index, and death benefit) a policy owner can adjust the policy to suit his financial needs, goals, and risk tolerance. For example, a retired person may want to eliminate market risk altogether by locking in a fixed interest rate.

The Indexed Universal Life policy limits the risk to the insurance company, and the policy owner, by imposing a 'ceiling' and a 'floor' on the policy owner's interest rate gain. For example; let's say the ceiling is 15% and the floor is 1%. If the market index goes up by 40% in the next year, the policy owner's gain is limited to 15% — to the insurance company's benefit. If, on the other hand, the market drops by 40%, the policy owner still gets 1%.

In theory, it appears that the policy cannot lose money. But be advised, that there are insurance company administrative costs that must be paid each month. If the policy floor is zero percent, and the market goes negative, those costs will be deducted from the cash value.

There is another parameter associated with the IUL called 'participation rate.' The participation rate is stated on the policy illustration, and on the policy itself. The participation rate is set at the insurance company's discretion. If the participation rate is 80%, then only 80% of the cash value is tied to a market. The other 20% has a fixed (low) interest rate.

By law, the insurance agent must provide you with an illustration, BEFORE he, or she, sells you any type of Universal life policy. A signed (by insurance agent and policy owner) illustration must be attached to the issued policy.

VARIABLE UNIVERSAL LIFE INSURANCE

VUL's have the same moving parts as IUL's. The major difference is RISK. VUL's don't have ceilings and floors. The policy owner's principal is invested Directly in a market, rather than being indexed. As a result, the policy owners cash value is exposed to the same risk and reward as the market. Remember, the greater the risk, the greater the reward. But you could, theoretical, lose your entire 'participating' cash accumulation. The participation rate will protect you from total collapse because a certain percent of the cash value is invested at a fixed rate interest.

These complex life insurance products can be difficult for a layperson to understand. If your insurance agent — your *licensed* insurance agent cannot explain the nature of the policy *to your satisfaction,* then don't buy the product. Period.

MIXED LIFE INSURANCE COVERAGE

Whole life insurance policies are expensive, compared to Term. But Term policies are not permanent. By combining Whole Life with Term Life coverage (Term plus Perm), you get the best of both worlds. Review the following chart.

Figure 20: The Game of Life

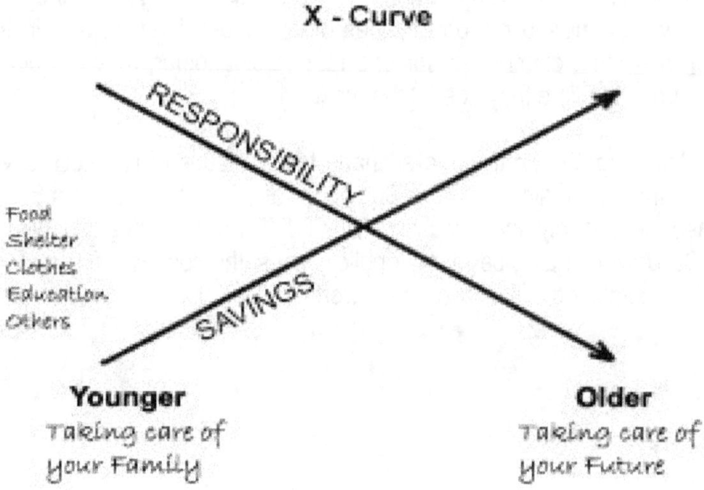

X - Curve

RESPONSIBILITY

Food
Shelter
Clothes
Education
Others

SAVINGS

Younger
Taking care of
your Family

Older
Taking care of
your Future

Most young families start out with little, or no savings. But they have the responsibility of providing for a growing family. They will often incur debt for things they cannot afford to buy with cash on hand. There will probably have at least one car note, and loans for furniture and appliances. Kitchen appliances are a must have.

At the same time, these parenting breadwinners are generally earning entry level salaries. The bills must be paid, no matter what. They cannot live without food, or gas to get to work. If both parents are working, there may eventually be childcare costs. There may be very little discretionary cash after the bills are paid. If one of the parents meets an early demise, the family's standard of living plunges to the depths of despair.

The family is shortsighted if they do not purchase life insurance to replace the decedents income. Whole Life is expensive. Term Life is affordable and easily understood. The policy should be designed to get the children to a point of self-sufficiency. The policy should cover college expenses for each child, if that is the parents' desire.

But term policies run out after the children are grown and on their way. A follow-on policy, of any type will be cost prohibitive. Most uninsured seniors wish they had purchased Whole Life insurance when they were young enough to afford it.

And, most seniors that are unprepared for retirement wished they'd started their retirement savings when they were much younger. In hindsight, they know they missed out on decades of compound interest. And in the case of those that didn't save, for one reason or another, they run out of money during the time they need it the most.

The following chart outlines a scenario for all stages of life. Let's say a family wishes to maintain $500,000 worth of life insurance. They can purchase a relatively inexpensive $250,000 Term Policy, along with a $250,000 Universal Life, permanent policy. Thus, the concept of Term Plus Perm. The combined initial coverage is worth $500,000.

Figure 21: Term Plus Perm

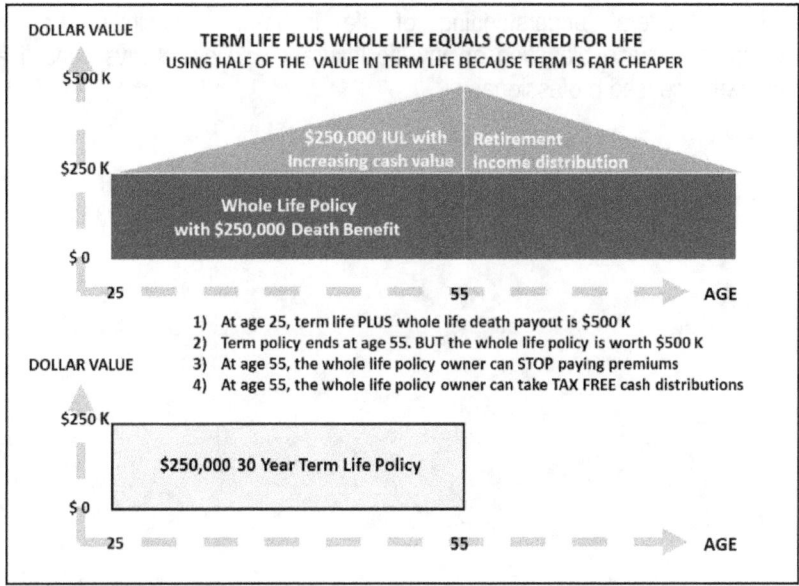

The objective is to have the Perm policy increase to $500,000 in coverage as the Term policy expires at retirement age. At this point the aging parents should have no parental responsibilities and zero debt. If there is a mortgage, it should be fully, or at least nearly paid off. The parents can then take tax free loan distributions and have life insurance coverage for life.

Optimally, the family may want to purchase two Term policies — one for each parent, and one Perm policy for the highest income earner, with another Perm policy for their spouse as soon as they are able. Remember, the sooner you start compound interest eligible savings, the longer the cash value will grow — and the larger it will grow.

SELF INSURANCE

If you are fortunate enough to have inherited a stable multigeneration fortune, you don't *need* life insurance at all. But you still may want to purchase a policy to cover your next generation's inheritance tax. And do remember that fortunes change. There is nothing permanent this side of eternity.

This concludes our discussion on life insurance. Do not consider this chapter to be all you need to know about life insurance. Our aim was to give you a general understanding of life insurance principles. For a comprehensive explanation of any life insurance policy, always consult a properly licensed professional.

CHAPTER 16: EMPLOYEE RETIREMENT PLANS

Employee retirement plans are structured to postpone or avoid Capital Gains taxation on retirement savings. There are many types. The tax deferred plans are paid for with pretax dollars. In other words, the government lets you plant your retirement investment without taxing your seed money. And they limit the amount you can contribute (reference table 6). And when your investment is mature, the government taxes the growth.

Table 6: Limits on Employee Retirements Contribution

Dollar Limits: 2019	
IRA Contribution	$6,000
If over age 50	$7,000
401(k) Contribution	$19,000
If over age 50	$25,000
SIMPLE IRA Contribution	$13,000
If over age 50	$16,000
SEP IRA Contribution	Lesser of $56,000 or 25% of Compensation
HSA Contribution (Individual)	$3,500
HSA Contribution (Family)	$7,000
Gift-Tax Exclusion	$15,000 per-recipient
Federal Estate Tax Exemption	$11.4 million per-spouse

Let's use an agricultural allegory. Tax deferred retirement plans are like buying a bushel of apple seeds for $400, tax free. But when the $40,000 apple crop comes in, you are taxed before you can sell them. Which would have been easier — paying tax on $400, or $40,000?

Table 7: Tax Deferred vs. Tax Free

Tax-deferred	Tax-free
IRA	Roth IRA
SEP IRA	Roth 401(k)
SIMPLE IRA	Roth 403(b)
401(k) & Profit Sharing	Roth 457
403(b)	529 Plan
457 Plan	Coverdell ESA
Qualified Annuity	Health Savings Account
Non-Qualified Annuity	

Tax free retirement plans are funded with after tax dollars. You pay taxes on the seed money, not on the mature cash crop. You must understand the difference before joining the plan. The federal and state tax on a million dollars could amount to nearly $400,000.

Your eligibility is dependent on many variables. Find an online diagram, similar to the one below to find a plan that fits your criteria.

Table 8: Employee Retirement Plan Characteristics

	Traditional IRA	Roth IRA	SEP IRA	SIMPLE IRA	401(k) / 403(b)
Annual contribution limit	$5,500 if you're under 50; $6,500 if you're 50 or older	$5,500 if you're under 50; $6,500 if you're 50 or older	25% of earnings, up to $54,000	$12,500 if you're under 50; $15,500 if you're 50 or older	$18,000 if you're under 50; $24,000 if you're 50 or older
Earliest withdrawal age to avoid penalties	59-½ (exceptions apply)	59-½ for earnings portion; principal contributions can be withdrawn at any time	59-½ (exceptions apply)	59-½ (exceptions apply)	59-½ (exceptions apply)
Required minimum distributions	Starting at 70-½	No required minimum distribution	Starting at 70-½	Starting at 70-½	Starting at 70-½
Taxes on contributions	Contributions are made with pre-tax dollars	Contributions are made with after-tax dollars	Contributions are made with pre-tax dollars	Contributions are made with pre-tax dollars	Contributions are made with pre-tax dollars
Taxes on withdrawals	Withdrawals are taxed as ordinary income	Withdrawals are tax-free	Withdrawals are taxed as ordinary income	Withdrawals are taxed as ordinary income	Withdrawals are taxed as ordinary income

Tax deferred plans may come with incentives to get you to take the tax deferred *bait*. Some plans have employer matching fund incentives. The company will match your contributions — up to a certain percent of your salary. But read the fine print carefully. There will probably be a step down in matching funds as you put more into the plan.

For example, the plan may say it matches 7% of your salary. But it may only be dollar for dollar, for the first 3%. Then 50 cents on the dollar for the next 2%, and 25 cents on the dollar for the last 2%. Read the plan features carefully. If you don't understand it, get someone from Employee Benefits to explain it to you. The company contributions and their growth will be taxed. The gains on your own contributions will be taxed. You can lower your tax burden at payout by taking smaller periodic withdrawals that put you in a lower tax bracket.

Finally, THESE ARE RETIREMENT PLANS. And thus, they are long term investments. You can, however, borrow against your account balance. But you will be paying back untaxed money with money that you pay taxes on. That defeats the purpose of the tax deferred investment. Besides paying taxes to replace the untaxed money, you will also pay interest on the loan. And in addition to that, the money that is loaned out to you is not drawing interest from the account. Borrowing money from your company retirement fund is a lose, lose, lose proposition.

CHAPTER 17: ANNUITIES

When it comes to life insurance, insurance companies want you to live to a ripe old age, so they can collect as many premium payments as possible. And you certainly don't want to die young, so your family can cash in on the policy. But there is an increasing chance, in light of modern medicine, that you may outlive your retirement savings.

ANNUITY

An annuity is defined as a sum of money paid to someone ANNually in perpetUITY. Meaning yearly — forever. Or, 12 payments per year, until the contract is fulfilled. By design, an annuity policy is a form of insurance entitling an investor to a series of annual sums.

Social Security is a personalized annuity payment funded by a government coffer that employees fill by having money deducted from their paychecks. The payroll deduction is mandatory. But you cannot receive the benefits unless you meet certain requirements. You must be closer to 70 years of than you are to 60. Or, you, or someone that makes you eligible, must die young or have a chronic illness. Accessing benefits under the latter circumstances can take years.

Through an annuity policy, you can fund your own *personal security* benefit that you can access at your own discretion. Before we go any further in this discussion, I want to make something crystal-clear. When you hear the words *'invest in an annuity'* — I want you to think of MONEY YOU WILL NOT HAVE TO TOUCH FOR SEVEN TO TEN YEARS. Annuities are strictly a long-term investment.

Why put money into an investment that will tie up your money for 7 to 10 years? So, you don't outlive your savings. You cannot work forever. But you can use part of your younger self's earnings to take care of your older self. You do not want to deplete your assets while you are still alive.

From the insurance companies' point of view, and annuity policy is the opposite of life insurance policy. In the case of life insurance, they hope you live to be 100 years old, so they can collect as many premium payments as possible. But with an annuity policy, they are betting that you die young, so they don't have to make payments to *you*, until you're 110 years old. Here's how it works.

PERSPECTUS

It is required, by law that you be given a detailed document — a prospectus, explaining the annuities working parts, PRIOR to signing an annuity contract. The insurance company must file the prospectus with the Security Exchange Commission (in most cases) prior to you signing the contract. Other government regulations apply in the case where the prospectus is not filed with the SEC. There are specific regulations that determine when, and how, the prospectus is presented to you — *and* what details it must contain. If you, or a trusted other, cannot understand the prospectus, then don't sign the annuity contract. Do not pretend to understand, if you don't.

ACCUMULATION PHASE

During the accumulation phase, you put money into the annuity, just like Social Security. You can put money, usually in equal sums monthly, annually, or all at once.

DISTRIBUTION PHASE

During distribution phase, the annuity pays you monthly payments — like an allowance. Distribution can be complicated. It can last, by your choice, for a fixed period. Or, you can receive payments as long as you live. There are distribution agreements that allow your beneficiary to continue collecting your payments or a fixed period. Or, in a lump sum death benefit.

Annuities are complex financial instruments, and not suited for people that are financially unstable, or financially naïve. There are several terms you will need to understand. The most important of which is the term 'annuitization.'

ANNUITIZATION

Annuitization is a noun that is a resultant of the verb annuitize. Once you ANNUITIZE the policy, the principal investment NO LONGER BELONGS TO YOU. It belongs to the insurance company. The insurance company is contractually obligated to make payments to you for the remainder of the agreed upon distribution period, or until you die.

Live a long time — you win. You can receive payments for the rest of your natural life, or for a shorter term of your choosing. If you die prematurely — the insurance company wins. They stop making payments, or they pay off your beneficiary. But your beneficiary does not inherit your payments for life.

Annuitization is complicated. But there is a way around giving your money over to the insurance company. You are allowed to take periodic withdrawals, typically up to 10% per year of the principal invested. However, if you do that, your investment will not grow. If you withdraw the maximum and your interest is less than that, your principal will decline.

Like universal life insurance, the annuity is tied — either to a fixed interest rate, a market indexed interest rate, or invested directly in the market.

PENALTIES FOR EARLY WITHDRAWAL

There are significant penalties for early withdrawal. Those penalties decrease annually, terminating at 7 to 10 years from signing the contract. If you cash out of the annuity in the first few years you will most likely lose money. That's because the early withdrawal penalty is likely to be more than the accrued interest.

ANNUITY UNDERWRITING

An insurance company, by law, cannot sell you an annuity unless you can prove that you are financially stable, and that you have other substantial liquid assets. If you are honest during the application process, the law will protect you. You should have adequate life insurance, an emergency fund, and discretionary cash to make the investment. That means money that you absolutely will not need for 7 to 10 years.

ANNUITANT

Like an insurance policy, the annuity contract is based on the life of a human being. That person is called the annuitant. The contract owner and the annuitant can be one in the same person, but they don't have to be. The contract owner and the beneficiary can be one and the same person, but they don't have to be. The owner, the annuitant, and the beneficiary can be three different people. The beneficiary can also be a trust.

IMMEDIATE ANNUITY

An immediate annuity is purchased with a single premium. And, annuitization takes place immediately. A person with verifiable discretionary cash may want to purchase an immediate annuity to receive distributions for a number of years, or for life. A million-dollar immediate annuity could easily generate $40,000 a year for life. In this case, the break-even point would be 25 years. There may even be a bonus for delaying the distribution for number of years. But you may regret giving a million dollars to an insurance company long before 25 years.

FIXED ANNUITY

A fixed annuity grows at a fixed interest rate. It is the simplest annuity to purchase, and the simplest to understand. They sometimes come with a yearly bonus, if you don't make any withdrawals for a fixed number of years. A fixed annuity avoids market risk. It's a sure thing, though the interest rate may only be a few percent. Lower risk — lower reward.

INDEXED ANNUITY

An indexed annuity, like the IUL, has an interest rate that is market indexed. Remember that there are annual management costs that will be deducted from your account whether you get interest rate growth, or not. Also, remember that past performance is no indication of future performance.

VARIABLE ANNUITY

A variable annuity has 'subaccounts' that may be invested, at your discretion, in different market segments. Keep in mind that diversity decreases non-systematic market risk. That is to say that unless the entire market takes a nose-dive, you will be protected against individual stock downturns. Proper diversification includes investments that typically go up when others typically go down. But, in theory you can lose all of your money. Even when the market is booming — past performance is not an indicator of future performance.

If you don't take away anything else from this chapter, remember that annuities are a long-term investment. In the long term, markets have traditionally gone up — on average 10% per year. It would be better if you are emotionally detached from any money invested in a variable annuity. There are bound to be market swings. If you cash out during a significant downturn, you lose. Otherwise, short-term losses are only paper losses.

A final warning. Annuities are highly complex financial instruments. Do not try to navigate these waters on your own. Always consult a competent licensed financial representative. And when it comes to annuities, I recommend you get more than one opinion.

CHAPTER 18: MUTUAL FUNDS

A mutual fund is a portfolio of shares, mutually owned by the constituent shareholders. The mutually owned fund is invested in the market at the discretion of the fund manager. There is a plethora of federal and state regulations that oversee the management and administration of these funds.

The advantages of aggregating the investments of a large group of people are numerous.

PROFESSIONAL MONEY MANAGEMENT

Most people take pride in a job well done. White-collar, blue-collar, or servant, we want to be known as one of the people in line for advancement. The more energy and excellence we put into our work, the likelier we are to earn a larger salary. And we are incentivized, through overtime pay, to work longer hours. Then at the end of the day, we give the last of our energy to our loved ones at home.

We stay in the rat race for decades, never learning much more than what it takes to support our family. Think about how long it took to get good at your job? How much time did you spend at work, to stay relevant in your field — or just to keep your job at all. If you knew a fourth as much about investing in stocks and bonds as you do about your career, you *might* be able to successfully navigate the stock market. But most likely you don't. When did you have time to learn?

The stock markets, by design, are complex and volatile. Money managers are required to be experts in large stock market portfolios. Why go it alone? Why take advise from your brother-in-law who doesn't know much more than you do? Financial services is one of the most highly regulated industries in the world. You either trust the system or end up squandering your assets based on the advice of laymen.

DIVERSIFICATION

Diversification is the key to a balanced portfolio. The fund manager will select individual stocks, bonds, money market instruments, and preexisting exchange traded funds. The fund manager is aware of the cyclical nature of certain market sectors; tech, durable goods, consumer staples, industrials, and so forth. The manager will balance the fund by buying contrary positions in those opposing sectors. People buy cars and boats in the summer, and natural gas to heat their homes in the winter. People purchase fad items from companies that are here today and gone tomorrow. But they always need soap and diapers.

In addition to sector diversity the manager can buy positions in several different global market exchanges. America, China, Japan, and Europe all have robust markets that operate somewhat independent of geographic trends.

Those markets are driven by interest rates. In America, markets are driven by the Federal Reserve Rate — that is the interest rate that banks charge other banks for overnight loans. When interest rates rise, bond prices increase. When interest rates go down, stocks become more attractive because investors are seeking a greater return.

If you are not a seasoned investor these trends may be foreign to you. Why would you gamble your savings on a game you are not equipped to play? Your competition — wall street investors, prey on naïve investors with emotional attachments to their money. When you panic and sell during a market collapse, there are billionaire sharks waiting to pick up your losses at fire sale prices. If all this information is new to you, you still know next to nothing. Therefore, mutual funds are attractive to unsophisticated investors.

BUYING POWER

Pooling your investment dollars with many other people allows you to compete with institutional investors. They get preferential treatment on the trading floor because they can leverage hundreds of millions of dollars. Big computer-generated block trades are serviced first. They'll get to your five thousand-dollar trade when they get to it. There are discounts for buying in bulk. Buy combining their money, mutual fund owners can potentially become market makers by trading in huge lots.

DAILY LIQUIDITY

Mutual funds can be bought and sold on a daily basis. But unlike stocks, bonds, and other exchange traded funds, Mutual funds trade at the daily closing price. You're not stuck in the investment for more than 24 hours. The intraday trading of the previously mentioned investments is done, for you, by a seasoned money manager.

Like annuities, mutual fund contracts are preceded by a prospectus which will tell you, specifically, which investments are contained in the overall fund. The prospectus will also show you fund's earnings track record. And thus, you can compare one fund to another's earnings performance.

Remember, if this is your first exposure to mutual funds, you are still a novice. You will need a properly licensed professional to explain the fund, the process, and to make the purchase on your behalf. Buying and selling based on emotion is still discouraged. Much greater knowledge of the financial landscape is baked into the stock market cake, so to speak. You won't outsmart the professional investors. You may get lucky, from time to time, making you feel as though you have a certain mojo. Even if you get lucky early in the game, when you finally lose, the loss will erase your lucky gains. Don't gamble — and that's what it is — with money you are sure to need in the near future. Enough said.

CHAPTER 19: BROKERAGE ACCOUNTS

Brokerage Accounts are held partly in the market and partly in a cash account with your name on it. It's your portfolio and your money. You can take cash out at any time, provided there is cash in the account. The brokerage account allows to convert stocks and other market investments to cash at any time. By doing so, you can take money out of the market when prices are up and buy more at a cheaper price when your investments go down.

MARKET TIMING

If you have tracked a cyclical stock and become aware of a seasonal pattern, you may anticipate peaks and valleys, selling high when the stock is up, and buying low when the stocks are down. But try not to become overly aggressive. Always leave a substantial portion of the brokerage account in cash.

If you sell out of a position when the stock is high, you will miss the opportunity for higher gains. If the stock never comes back down, you will be priced out of the market. Resist the urge to buy at a higher price than you sold. Conversely, if you spend your investible cash on a stock when you think it's low, and it goes lower, you may get stuck in an investment that may never recover.

DOLLAR COST AVERAGING

A better way to beat the market and gain ground is through Dollar Cost Averaging. The math says that if you periodically put equal sums of money in the same variable investment, the average cost of the purchases will be less than the average price of the investment.

Say, for example, you purchased a hundred dollars' worth of a particular varying stock every month for 12 months, your average cost per share will be less than the average price the stock sold for during that year.

It works because that same hundred dollars buys more shares when the price is down. And when the price is higher, you're still only spending one hundred dollars. Conversely, if you buy the same number of shares per month, you would have to be lucky to purchase shares at less the average price. With dollar cost averaging the math guarantees it.

SELF DIRECTED BROKERAGE ACCOUNTS

Anyone can sign up for a Self-Directed Brokerage Account. There are several companies that provide this service. You deposit the cash, and *you* choose the investment. And though you cannot technically complete the trade, *you* have trading authority. Simply call the company, or go to their website, and specify what you want to buy or sell — and when.

You can invest or divest, by dollar amount or by the number of shares. But since your money is not pooled with big money, your trade will not have priority. Computerized trades go first, big money — noncomputerized goes next. Your trade happens when it's convenient for the trading process. But Self-Directed accounts are cheaper because they have no management fees.

Market Order

A market order is an order to buy, or sell, a position at the current market price. As long as there is someone who is willing to sell what you want to buy — or buy what you want to sell, the market order is filled at the first executable opportunity. Market orders are used when certainty of execution is a priority over the price of execution. A market order is the simplest of the order types.

Buy Stop Order

Your stop order instructs a broker to purchase a security when it hits a strike price that is higher than the current spot price. Once the price hits that strike, your buy stop becomes a market order, fillable at the next available price. This type of order can apply to stocks, derivatives, or a variety of other tradable instruments. The buy stop order is based on the underlying assumption that a share price will continue to rise after the order is placed.

Buy Limit Order

A buy limit order is an order to purchase an asset at or below a specified price, allowing traders to control how much they pay. By using a buy limit order, the investor is guaranteed to pay that price or less. While the price is guaranteed, the filling of the order is not. If the asset does not reach the specified price, the order is not filled, and the investor may miss out on the trading opportunity. Said another way, by using a buy limit order the investor is guaranteed to pay the buy limit order price or lower. But it is not guaranteed that the order will be filled.

Sell Stop Order

A stop order (or stop-loss order) is an order to sell a stock when the price of the stock reaches the stop price. You specify the stop price. When the stop price is reached, the stop order becomes a market order. A sell stop order is entered at a stop price below the current market price. Investors generally use a sell stop order to limit a loss or to protect a profit on a stock that they own.

Sell Limit Order

Stop-limit orders are similar to stop-loss orders, but as the name states, there is a limit on the price at which they will execute. There are two prices specified in a stop-limit order: the stop price, which will convert the order to a sell order, and the limit price. Instead of the order becoming a market order to sell, the sell order becomes a limit order that will only execute at the limit price or better.

Figure 22: Stops and Limits

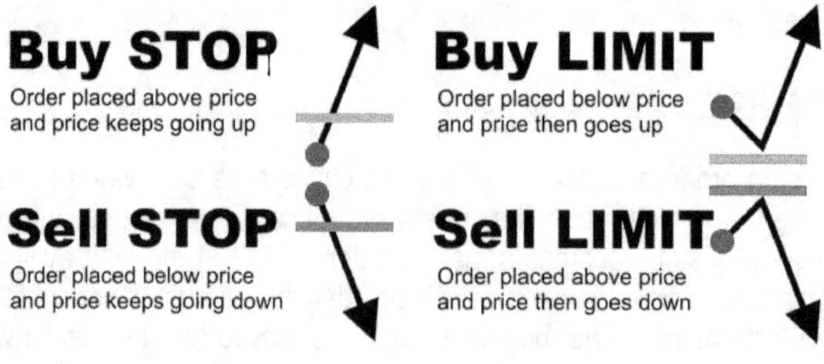

Buy STOP
Order placed above price
and price keeps going up

Buy LIMIT
Order placed below price
and price then goes up

Sell STOP
Order placed below price
and price keeps going down

Sell LIMIT
Order placed above price
and price then goes down

MANAGED BROKERAGE ACCOUNTS

For a competitive fee, you can open a brokerage account with a properly licensed Financial Management Firm. In that case, a professional money manager will evaluate your current financial situation — a sort of a financial checkup akin to a medical examination. By this means they will determine the investment strategy that is best suited to your individual needs.

A that point, a Financial Advisor will discuss your case with you, and if you agree, he or she will make recommendations. If you decide to open a brokerage account with them, they will choose a portfolio consisting of stocks, bonds, mutual funds, exchange traded funds and so forth. A Portfolio Manager will oversee your accounts, and if given trading authority they will buy and sell positions to keep your portfolio balanced. Through this oversight the Portfolio Manager will keep the different segments proportional to the initial strategic allocation.

CHAPTER 20: MARGIN ACCOUNTS

A Margin Account uses leverage as an investment strategy by using borrowed money, or borrowed stocks, to increase the potential return of an investment. These accounts are not for entry level investors — period. You can lose money that you don't even have. In a leveraged account you can also prearrange and preapprove certain market actions and specific price points.

Options

Options give you a right to take some sort of action by a predetermined date. That right is the buying or selling of shares of the underlying stock. Exercising that right is not mandatory.

The two types of options are Calls and Puts. And there are two sides to every option transaction. One party buys the option, and the other party sells the option. The seller writes the option. Both sides have advantages and disadvantages. The buyer of the option has a *long* position. He or she hopes to take advantage of the option by exercising their right. The seller of the option has a *short* position. They hope that they can make money selling the option without the buyer being in a position to exercise their right.

You must be some kind of guru to buy or sell options. The Options market does not allow novices to participate. Writing an option is akin to selling horses that won't win the race. Buying an option is like buying a cheap horse that *will* win.

Put

A Put option is a contractual obligation to buy an investment from the buyer of the Put. The Put buyer holds the long position and will exercise his sell option if the Put price is higher than the market price. The seller of the Put holds the short position and charges the buyer a nonrefundable premium for the Put — in hopes that the market price will remain higher than the Put price for the contract period. If it does, the seller of the Put gains the price of the premium. If not, he or she must buy the investment at the contractual price.

Call

A Call option is a contractual obligation to sell a position to the buyer of the Call. The Call buyer holds the long position and will exercise his buy option if the Call price is lower than the market price. The seller of the Call holds the short position and charges the buyer a nonrefundable premium for the Call — in hopes that the market price will remain lower than the Call price for the contract period. If it does, the seller of the Call gains the price of the premium. If not, he must sell the investment at the contractual price. And he or she is obligated to do so, even if they don't have it in their possession. In that case they would have to buy at the higher market price and sell at the Call price. That action is called an uncovered call. There is no limit to what a seller of the call could lose.

Figure 23: Options Matrix

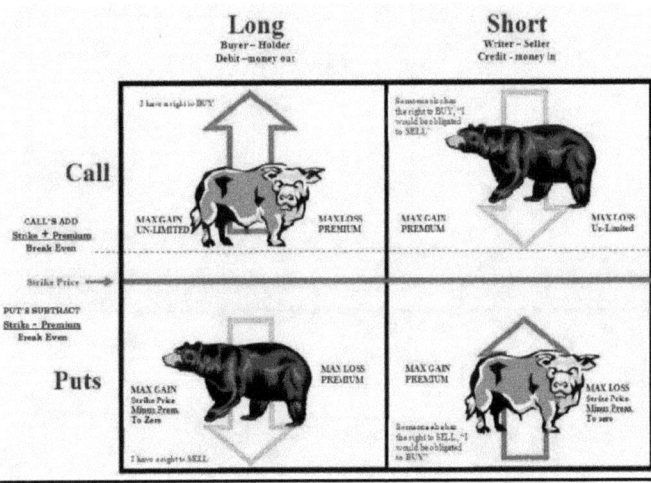

In no way presume or assume that this elementary introduction to Options or any other financial instrument is a recommendation or training. We do not guarantee this information to be correct in every detail. We only wished to show that high finances can be a minefield that you do not want to navigate alone.

It might be better to keep your investments limited to that which you can thoroughly understand. There are books or courses that can help you understand these products. But, ultimately, if you can't understand a product — DON'T BUY IN!

CHAPTER 21: HEDGE FUNDS

If you understood Hedge funds, you wouldn't be reading this book in the first place. A Hedge fund is a limited partnership of investors that use high risk methods, such as investing with borrowed money, in hopes of realizing large capital gains.

Hedge fund managers are, for lack of better terminology, super-brainiacs. They create complex automated algorithms to stay ahead of other traders, in hopes of beating the market. They are the wolves of Wall Street.

Hedge fund investments are not for the faint of heart. It takes a lot of money to buy in. You cannot make withdrawals. And you may be asked to put in more money. Your financial acumen must be vetted, before you are allowed to participate.

You will not understand this investment, aside from the rules of engagement. If you did, you'd already be making a killing in the market. You would have no reason to be reading this book.

If you have ten million dollars to bet on one number on the Roulette Wheel, you could participate in a Hedge fund. Or, just place a ten million dollar bet on one number on the Roulette Wheel. You might be better off buying ten million lottery tickets. Then you'd be likely to recoup some of your investment. If a Hedge fund fails, your money is gone.

CHAPTER 22: REITS

Real Estate Investment Trusts — REIT's are similar to mutual funds, in that investors combine their capital to venture into real estate investments. Income is earned proportional to each investor's contribution. A REIT's taxable income is paid out as dividends to shareholders. Shareholders pay income tax on those dividends.

There are three main types of REITs: equity REITs, mortgage REITs, and hybrid REITs. Equity REITs own, operate, and trade hard real estate assets. Mortgage REITs trade commercial and residential mortgages, and hybrid REITs are a combination of equity and mortgage REITs. The majority of revenue associated with equity REITs comes from real estate property rent. The revenue associated with mortgage REITs is generated from interest through mortgage loans.

Investments in REITs have their benefits and drawbacks. The benefits of investing in REITs include their lower investment entry costs. REITs can be purchased little as $500 for the price of one share.

If a REIT that you invested in fails, you may not get any of your money back. But on the other hand, you will not be responsible for any debt if you are not a managing partner.

CHAPTER 23: INDEPENDENT SAVINGS

Your overall investment strategy should be one that insures your financial stability for the rest of your life. Social Security has been a retirement subsidy for many Americans. But the future of Social Security is uncertain, because it is funded by younger workers supporting retirees. That worked fine when there were enough young workers to support an aging population. However, the baby boomer generation broke the business model. There are not enough workers to support the largest aging population in American history.

Employees are often comforted because they have terrific benefits at their job. Because of that, they fail to make a plan that is independent of the job. Jobs come and go. And with them go the benefits. Some of those benefits may be portable from a group plan, to a private plan. But you lose the group rates.

You should always consider the benefits in the company plan. In some instances, it's literally free money. The following diagram is but an example of an independent life-long financial strategy — a plan that stays in place whether you have employee benefits or not.

Figure 24: Independent Investment House

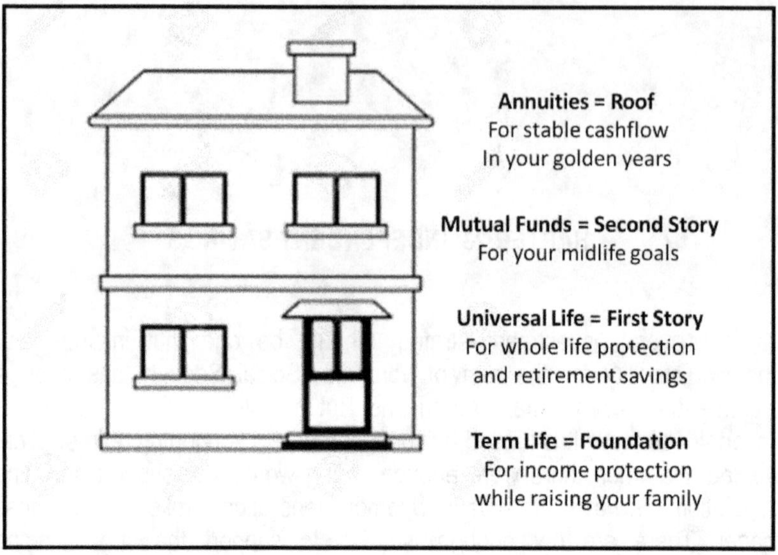

Annuities = Roof
For stable cashflow
In your golden years

Mutual Funds = Second Story
For your midlife goals

Universal Life = First Story
For whole life protection
and retirement savings

Term Life = Foundation
For income protection
while raising your family

This was but an example and should not be considered as any type of recommendation. Always consult a properly licensed professional to help you build your independent financial plan.

The professional consultation should begin with a series of standard questions. This is to ensure that any particular product is suitable to your particular situation. There are Federal and State regulations — laws in place to protect you from predatory recommendations. But you must be honest with your Agent, Representative, or Advisor.

The watch word is DON'T. If you don't understand the product, don't buy in. Company benefits are well regulated and easily explained. But make sure you understand them, for there may be exorbitant tax ramifications in the future.

And finally, your financial services professional IS NOT a tax professional. They cannot and should not be giving you tax advice. Always consult a tax expert — not cousin Susie — while formulating your estate plan.

This section on Financial Products has in no way been completely comprehensive. We are not responsible for you acting on any of this information. Consider it a general overview of some of the financial tools available to you.

DISCLAIMER: The information provided in SECTION TWO of "THE DEBT TRAP" is intended to provide general information only. And the information has been prepared without taking into account any particular person's objectives, financial situation or needs. Before acting on such information, you should consider the appropriateness of the information, your personal objectives, financial situation or needs. In particular, you should obtain professional advice before acting on the information contained on this section.

No representation or warranty is made as to the accuracy, completeness or reliability of any estimates, opinions, conclusions or other information contained in this section. This section may contain certain positive statements. Positive statements are not guarantees of future performance. The products discussed involve known and unknown risks, uncertainties and other factors. You should not place reliance on positive statements.

To the maximum extent permitted by law, we disclaim all liability and responsibility for any direct or indirect loss or damage which may be suffered as a result of relying on anything in this section, including any positive statements. Past performance is not an indication of future performance.

CHAPTER 23: THE GREATEST INVESTMENT

I'm about to discuss the wisest investment you could ever make. But before we start, understand that this principle has been proven over and over in my own life. By avoiding debt and investing in this basic truth, my family has never been without. We have been close to the brink but have never fallen into ruin. We have toyed with the idea of chasing worldly pleasure but chose not to. Such pursuits would only end in folly.

There is an investment that has always paid off! This principle rule, and its results, far exceeds the worldly standards of wealth and all the rest of the levels of wealth talked about earlier in the book. What is this basic principle? What is this wise investment? In a word — LOVE.

First Corinthians Chapter Thirteen

"If I speak in the tongues of men and of angels, but I do not have love, I am a noisy gong or a clanging cymbal. And if I have prophecy, and know all mysteries and all knowledge, and if I have all faith so that I can remove mountains, but do not have love, I am nothing. If I give away everything I own, and if I give over my body in order to boast, but do not have love, I receive no benefit. Love is patient, love is kind, it is not envious. Love does not brag; it is not puffed up. It is not rude, it is not self-serving, it is not easily angered or resentful. It is not glad about injustice but rejoices in the truth. It bears all things, believes all things, hopes all things, endures all things. Love never fails."

Most people think that the passage is just for marital relations. But I assure you it's for all of them. Even if you don't believe the way that I do, reading that passage will give you a very clear definition of love, as it could, and should be. But at the end of that there's a statement that is often forgotten — LOVE NEVER FAILS.

Right there in black and white — the guarantee that this investment will never fail. What a blessed assurance. If only we could remember that in all circumstances. Even with all the work I've done, I'm still not quite there yet, but I'm a work in progress.

God also gave us a clear outline of how to summarize all of his concepts about love and goodness with one simple statement the golden rule. It is "to love God with all your heart soul mind and strength and your neighbor as yourself". If we can do this financially, spiritually, mentally, and physically our wealth will be assured.

So, the first part of the golden rule is what we should do, the second part of the golden rule is how we should do it. So, if I actually love God with all my heart soul and mind, I will show that by loving my neighbor as myself. And when we say neighbor, we mean your family, your immediate neighbors, your coworkers, and anyone else in your sphere of influence.

If we devote ourselves to treating people as we want to be treated when we are wrong, or make mistakes, or sin, or say something insensitive, then we have invested in wealth in a way that the greedy never will. Think about the times when you made a mistake and how people treated you. It may have been okay that they got angry because anger is God-given and good. But how did you feel when they stepped into judgment and wrath?

List below, some of the mistakes that you've made, who it affected. Then add how their wrathful response caused even more damage. Then add how your response to their wrath escalated the discourse. Then ask yourself, was yours a response that came out of love, or not?

Mistake: _____
Who it Affected: _____
Their Response: _____
Your Response: _____
Loving or not: _____

Mistake: _____
Who it Affected: _____
Their Response: _____
Your Response: _____
Loving or not: _____

Mistake: _____
Who it Affected: _____
Their Response: _____
Your Response: _____
Loving or not: _____

This change of heart will tie back into financial success. How do you want to be treated when you make mistakes? Do you treat people that way when they make mistakes? If not, then your job will be to model the behavior by which you want other people to treat you. If we can become proficient in this practice, we can remove half the fears that cause us to make unwise investments. Love never fails. Never. NEVER. Remember that.

The other half of our fears can be removed by listing the people, places, and things that have injured us, financially. When we perceive those threats in our current environment, we fear those injuries happening again. If we can step away from those fears and act with the principles of loving mercy, we can avoid the financial mistakes that lead to debt. We will act out of wisdom instead of fear.

Our desires to be appreciated, loved, and respected are as basic as human necessities such as water, shelter, and human contact. But because we filter these needs through our fears, we react in ways that take us further away from those God-given needs. We then isolate ourselves in what may be a comfortable environment, but certainly not a blessed and prosperous one.

Let's address these fears and injuries objectively. List below, the people that have injured you, what they did, your reaction — positive, negative, loving or fearful? Then think about how you could have reacted more lovingly. How could you have treated them the way you would've wanted to be treated?

Who/what committed the injury: _____
What was the injury: _____
Your response: _____
A more appropriate response: _____

Who/what committed the injury: _____
What was the injury: _____
Your response: _____
A more appropriate response: _____

Who/what committed the injury: _____
What was the injury: _____
Your response: _____
A more appropriate response: _____

Looking at these, objectively, we can eliminate reactions that might end up costing us. And putting ourselves in holes that we may never dig ourselves out of — spiritually, physically, emotionally, or financially. We should focus on what love does, and how to model that behavior for others. Then we can avoid the costly circumstances altogether. Because love never fails.

When I get angry, my first instinct is still to be wrathful, because I'm hurt. Instead of that initial response, I pause and give myself a minute to pray and meditate about what just happened. I find out why I'm angry, and then go back and try to have an objective conversation. That pause allows me to be honest about who I am and how I feel. And it gives the other person the opportunity to respond appropriately, or not.

If I don't express how I feel, I become resentful, and the angst stays in me like a poison. Carrying a resentment toward somebody is like drinking poison and hoping the other person suffers. Lovingly expressing the injury and allowing the other person their own thoughts, feelings, ideas and expressions resolves most of the matters right then and there, with no financial consequences.

I can illustrate exactly why loving your neighbors as yourself is the wisest financial investment you can ever make. In this first chart each circle represents you or somebody in your life, with you being at the center.

Figure 25: Shared Wealth

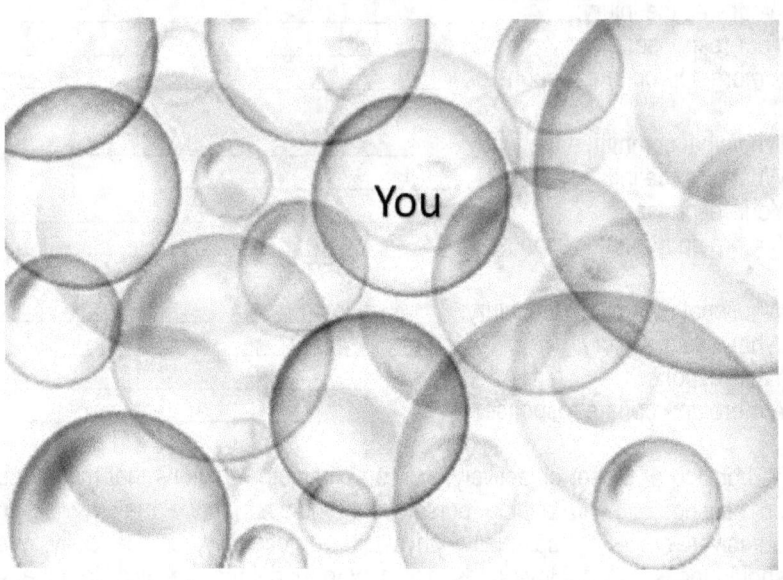

You may not have the biggest circle of stuff. All the people around you have the same size circle or close to it. But everybody's circle is fully attached — or dare I say that the circle of influence between you and your neighbors is full integrity. I want you to envision those circles as a fortress of protection around you. Because your circle of influence has full integrity, you and others are protected from damage caused by outside influences?

If you invest your resources, and time, into making sure your family and neighbors are strong and secure, or at least as strong and secure as you, then two things happen. First, because they are all strong and well-equipped, they will defend and protect your interests, like they were their own, because indeed they are. Secondly, because they are strong and secure, they have no need or desire to try to take what you have in order to feed their own families.

If you love on your neighbors and make them secure, you train them how to do that with their neighbors. Then your area of security expands — not just to your neighbors; it keeps expanding through your community. Your community then expands the love-modeled behavior through your city. Your city model expands through your state, your state through your country, and so on.

The main function of our Democratic Republic is supposed to be to encourage and enable us to do this exact thing. It is supposed to protect our right and ability to thrive, from greedy, fearful people that seek to strip us of our resources and take away our right and ability to protect ourselves from their greed.

You can see, through the previous illustration, that love applied to the principles of wealth will lead to long-term stability for you and everybody you love. Guaranteed — love never fails.

Now let's look at the opposite illustration where sin rules and people live in fear. Greedy people try to hoard all the resources to themselves, at the expense of everybody else around them.

Figure 26: BIG YOU – little them

They build for massive houses and fences with full security to keep people from getting to them. Why? Because the people around them live in lack. *They* have money socked away in offshore accounts, to protect their ill-gotten gains. *They* keep two sets of books to hide their dirty deals. And *they* live in constant fear of retaliation from those they've harmed.

By draining the resources of their friends, family, neighbors, city, state and country, and leaving them in lack, they actually create the very situation they fear. The people beneath the greedy person don't have the ability or desire to defend the greedy person. The greedy person becomes trapped in their own bubble.

Since fear, and the manifestations there of, are the leading cause of debt; how do we get around it.? How do we leave fear behind and march confidently into a new financial freedom? It ties back to the golden rule. If you have an issue with God, just put that part aside if you choose to. But I strongly suggest you hear me out.

Because I choose to love God with all my heart, soul, mind and strength and my neighbor as myself — I have to try to view myself and my neighbors the way God does. I choose to serve Jesus, because after studying all the different gods out there, He was the only one that had historical, moral, and powerful solutions to fear. He also didn't care where you came from or what you looked like. He didn't care about your history or your failures. He only cared that you knew that God loved you, and that He would do everything in His power to prove it.

With that as my example for love, I must seek to tear down my own insecurities and fears — my own limited understanding of people, places, and things. I must try to see people the way that God does and love them unconditionally. Unfortunately, I have not been given an on/off switch. It takes work.

This is the work that it takes. First, I must list everybody that has harmed me, objectively looking at what they did to hurt me, and then ask myself: what was my part in it? Was I operating out of fear, or faith? Was I being selfish or dishonest? This I must do, on a continual basis, to illuminate my own unloving attitudes, and stay in a place where I don't have to waste my money or time building walls between myself and others. I must come to realize that there is no one greater than me, and no one lesser.

Some people have to look way deeper to find God. But He will reveal Himself if we earnestly seek Him.

Below, list: (1) the people that have angered you, and you are still carrying the hurt. Then (2) list what they did. Then (3) list how it affected you. When you see how it affected you, I want you to consider your ambitions. Did it affect your financial ambitions? Your social status? Your sexual ambitions? Your health and welfare? And then lastly (4) list your part in the hurtful situation. Were you trying to be a good husband, wife, mother, father, daughter, son, neighbor, family member, citizen, or friend? Or, were you just selfish or self-centered, trying to get more than your share of whatever you were seeking? Are you a hypocrite? Do you exhibit the same behavior to others, that was hurtful to you? Try one example, using the situation you resent the most.

Who hurt me: _____
How they hurt me: _____
How it affected me: _____
What was my part: _____

Were you expecting people to behave in ways that would've been disproportionately favorable to *you*? Were you hoping for people to be something different than their behavior has shown you to be? Were you dishonest with them either directly or indirectly? Try it again, with a different situation, searching your heart for the truth this time.

Who hurt me: _____
How they hurt me: _____
How it affected me: _____
What was my part: _____

I considered myself to be a very honest person, but when I went through this process, I realized just how dishonest I was — even with myself. By justifying my own agenda, I created a snowball at the top of my pious mountain, that rolled down and grew, crushing me when I fell to the bottom. Try it again, being even more honest with yourself.

Who hurt me: _____
How they hurt me: _____
How it affected me: _____
What was my part: _____

Unfortunately, I was still expecting people to read my mind and respond appropriately when I was angry. But how could they, when my real motives were a secret. Try it one last time, with the most honesty you can muster.

Who hurt me: _____
How they hurt me: _____
How it affected me: _____
What was my part: _____

By now you should clearly see that you are not perfect. You should see that your own hidden motives can harm other people. And knowing that, you must allow grace to other people who are just as human as you are. If not, you will blunder on, full of hypocrisy and spite. For by the same measure you judge, you will be judged.

You may or may not ever want these people back in your life. And either way it's okay. But if they are living in your head *rent-free*, then that anger is rolling around in your head and your heart. Just like drinking poison and hoping the other person is going to die. We have to be free of this in order to be free of the decisions that bring us to financial devastation.

Now let's look at this list from a different perspective. I must, can, and will forgive the other party for their offense. But how can I do that without allowing the offense to happen again? Good question. Forgiveness does not mean allowing the other person to continue to harm you. You may be well justified to keep your distance from those people. Forgiveness is just giving up your right to revenge. Forgiveness is understanding that one will reap what they sow. Have pity on those who still do what *you* used to do. Pray for them that still live in greed and fear. This is the first step in truly being able to love.

As a result of this process, I learned how to check my own motives before I engaged in transactions with other people — especially financial transactions. And I learned to apologize when I was wrong. To be free from costly fear we must look objectively at the people, places, or institutions that we have harmed, and become willing to make amends to them all. Not just saying I'm sorry but making things right — no matter the cost.

This is the process by which we can forgive ourselves and let go of the destructive behaviors that put us in debt. When talking about amends we're talking about mending something that is torn. Restoring that item, person, as best we can to the undamaged condition they were in before we harmed them. If we are to walk free from fear and be able to make decisions on sound principles, then this is a must.

Just because we are willing to make amends, doesn't mean we ought to rush right out and do it. In some cases, it is better to discuss your offenses with a trusted friend, lawyer, or clergyman that can give you sound counsel. List here the people, places, and things you have harmed. Then list what your behavior cost them. And, finally, resolve to make it right as soon as possible.

Who I hurt: _____
How I hurt them: _____
How it affected them: _____
How I will make them whole: _____

Who I hurt: _____
How I hurt them: _____
How it affected them: _____
How I will make them whole: _____

Who I hurt: _____
How I hurt them: _____
How it affected them: _____
How I will make them whole: _____

Once you have cleared away the wreckage of your financial past, you will be free of worry and fear. You will live in a new light, with clear vision — inviting God into all of your financial relationships. And you will be able to reach back and pull someone else out of the clutches of the debt trap.

Showing love to your family, friends, and neighbors is the best financial investment you can ever make. In doing so you make them strong and secure. Then they will fight for your security as well. This is God's simple wisdom of financial freedom through charitable stewardship in the covenant church.

The End

ABOUT THE AUTHOR

John R. Champion has distilled seven years of research, dedication, and in-the-trenches experience to understand the Debt Trap. John can help you break the trap so you and your family will never get caught in it again.

His first exposure to the debt and credit hamster wheel, exhausting nearly every American, was actually through reading the Bible. As a young man, John prayed for the wisdom of Solomon.

Since that time, he has dedicated himself to the study of the Word, to dependence on Jesus Christ, and to the communities he has lived in. His reputation of integrity, objectivity, and clarity precedes him in the business, spiritual, and financial worlds.

John currently owns three business's dedicated to helping people make decisions based on their spirit and character, rather than their bank account. He is a broker, and an expert in credit monitoring and repair, and debt negotiation. He also carries a license for life and health insurance.

He has been a dedicated husband and father to our four children. He Serves as a Deacon at his church and has dedicated much of his time to helping people recover from drug and alcohol addiction.

With thirty years' experience in sales, John has mastered the art of listening, teaching, and connecting the people he serves. He knows the avenues to get them what they need (and often want)!

Combining his wisdom from the worlds of sales and finance, John has penned an easy to read, enlightening handbook dedicated to your personal journey of achieving your financial freedom.

This book marks a new milestone in his personal journey and in his message to the body of Christ. Please enjoy!

— Hope Champion

Mr. Champion can be reached for consultation, at 951-523-7850. Or email him at hopeinspiredfp@gmail.com.

www.ingramcontent.com/pod-product-compliance
Lightning Source LLC
LaVergne TN
LVHW051602070426
835507LV00021B/2730